AFFECTIVE EDUCATION:

A Methods and Techniques Manual for Growth

James D. Wiggins
University of Delaware
and
Dori English
New Castle-Gunning Bedford School District

Copyright © 1979 by
University Press of America, Inc.™
4710 Auth Place, S.E., Washington, D.C. 20023

All rights reserved
Printed in the United States of America

ISBN: 0-8191-0217-2

PREFACE

This manual is for educators searching for practical ways of helping pupils to explore and learn more about human feelings, needs, and behavior - searching for ways to humanize their classrooms. It is not a specific curriculum to be followed; rather, it is a compilation of strategies, activities, and procedures which may serve as models or examples as you begin an affective education program. The authors believe that your creativity and experience will then help you to develop your own "affective curriculum."

This manual should not be read like a book. You may wish to examine the table of contents and begin reading the sections that seem most interesting. However, reading is not enough! We hope you will try some of the suggested activities with your children. Don't be afraid to tell the children you are experimenting and learning yourself. Also, it might be helpful to work together with another teacher. Then, you can encourage, support, and offer feedback to each other.

THE STATE BOARD OF EDUCATION

Albert H. Jones, Christiana, President
Richard M. Farmer, New Castle, Vice-President
Robert W. Allen, Seaford
Charles C. Brown, Dover
Mrs. Lula Cooper, Hockessin
Mrs. Elise Grossman, Wilmington
Robert H. McBride, Wilmington

OFFICERS OF THE DEPARTMENT OF PUBLIC INSTRUCTION
Townsend Building
Dover, Delaware 19901

Kenneth C. Madden, State Superintendent
Ervin C. Marsh, State Administrative Assistant
Randall L. Broyles, Assistant State Superintendent
    Instructional Services Branch
Howard E. Row, Assistant State Superintendent
    Auxiliary Services
John J. Ryan, Assistant State Superintendent
    Administrative Services

TABLE OF CONTENTS

	PAGE
INTRODUCTION	1
MERGING FEELING ORIENTED AND FACT ORIENTED LEARNING THROUGH DISCUSSIONS	8
BRINGING FEELINGS, EMOTIONS, NEEDS, AND HUMAN BEHAVIOR INTO THE CURRICULUM.	10
Merging Affective and Cognitive Areas	10
TRANSLATING IDEAS INTO ACTIONS: SELF-TEACHING ACTIVITIES	22
ACTIVITIES TO ENHANCE PUPIL DISCUSSION SKILLS	37
Affective and Cognitive Intergration Summary.	44
The Use of Critical Discussion Strategies & Discussion Technique: A Summary	44
ACTIVITIES TO BRING THE AFFECTIVE DOMAIN INTO THE CLASSROOM.	46
Introduction	46
1. 1 Warm-Ups--Pantomining Events, Actions, and Feelings	48
1. 2 Mirroring	50
1. 3 Blind Journey	51
1. 4 "Seeing" Without Your Eyes.	53
1. 5 Jungle Symphony	54
1. 6 Group Puzzle Activity	55
1. 7 Interviewer	57
1. 8 Counselor	58
1. 9 Who Is It?	60
1.10 Who Am I?	61
1.11 Seeing--Feeling Glasses	63

		PAGE
1.12	But I Cant't Be Me	65
2. 1	About Me	69
2. 2	Follow Up to "About Me"	71
2. 3	What Will I Be	72
2. 4	What I Am Like	73
2. 5	Me and School	75
2. 6	How I Am With People In My Class	77
2. 7	What Is Important to Me	80
2. 8	Friends - What I Do For Them and What They Do For Me	81
2. 9	Other People and Me	83
2.10	The Powers I Have--Self Control	84
2.11	The Powers I Have--Using Words	86
2.12	The Powers I Have--If I Were The King	88
2.13	The Powers I Have--Group Pressure	90
2.14	This Was The Week That Was	92
2.15	Telegram	94

GETTING LESSONS STARTED: SOME GUIDELINES 105

DEALING WITH MISBEHAVIOR BY INCREASING RESPONSIBILITY
AND PARTICIPATION. 122

SOME ILLUSTRATIONS 130

    Illustration 135

INTRODUCTION

Why should we concern ourselves at all with the affective realm of a child's development? To answer this, we must examine the meaning of affective education. The major concern of affective education is the healthy emergence and acceptance of a child's feelings and needs. It is this crucial emotional growth that enables each child to accept and understand self and others and gives one control over personal learning behavior. Without this, the child is crippled when attempting the cognitive learning tasks presented in school.

Educators have had a long struggle in dealing with children who somehow seem "unable" or "unwilling" to learn. Such children may become, through their own frustration or the frustration of their teachers, behavior problems in elementary school or dropouts in high school. The school has failed both these children and the society in which they are unprepared to live. The school failed, not because it was unconcerned but because it did not recognize an essential part of learning, affective development.

This manual is dedicated to the need for, and application of, affective education. It recognizes the worth of feelings and human behavior, explores the possibilities of improving the classroom learning climate, ways to merge affective and cognitive learning, and offers activities that encourage affective growth. Such an approach to education enhances the development of every child.

Affective education strives to enhance the development of the global objectives of self-esteem, understanding of self and others, and self-discipline.

There are more specific objectives that may be accomplished during one or two years of affective education programming. Following are some examples of what children could learn through classrooms that focus on the feeling as well as the knowing sides of learning.

A. Pupils may <u>increase</u> their <u>awareness and understanding</u> of human feelings, needs, and behavior. They may:
   1. be better able to understand the feelings of themselves and others.
   2. become more aware of their basic emotional and psychological needs and how these needs represent a common bond among all people.
   3. become more aware of how the behavior of self and others can help in meeting basic emotional needs.
   4. become more aware of how the behavior of others influences their own feelings and how their own behavior influences the feelings of others.
   5. learn to understand their personal needs and unique characteristics.

B. Pupils may develop more effective group and interpersonal <u>communication</u> skills such as:
   1. a desire and ability to listen carefully to other children.
   2. a desire and ability to clearly express one's feelings and opinions.

3. the ability to complete small group discussions with little adult supervision.
4. the ability to communicate acceptance and support of their peers.

C. Pupils may develop more effective group and interpersonal interaction skills such as:
1. learning to approach all human relations problems through rational discussion.
2. becoming more accepting of individual differences and less willing to deny the feelings and needs of others.
3. developing feelings of responsibility to other people and themselves.
4. becoming interested in teaching other children and helping their peers.
5. attempting to help specific children rather than ridicule or ignore them.
6. becoming more aware of the choices they have regarding their behavior and peer interaction.
7. feeling free to creatively express and explore fields of interest.

Even this incomplete list of objectives is quite varied. It is also obvious that affective education is potentially as valuable for all children, not just those with behavior problems. Indeed, low self-esteem, feelings of being isolated from peers and adults, and feelings of powerlessness are often viewed as underlying determinants of disruptive behavior, aggressive behavior, attention seeking, withdrawal, and various other school behavior problems. If these negative feelings do underline problem behavior, then a relevant question is: "What can be done to enhance children's feelings of esteem, togetherness, and worth?" While the mastery of academic and physical skills partially answers this question, a systematic emphasis on affective education is an additional response. Affective education is not meant to replace more traditional learning objectives and activities, but rather should be viewed as an additional set of considerations valuable for all children.

The Classroom Climate: Messages We Convey to Children

Regardless of what we are teaching, we are always sending messages to children by the way we approach, respond to, and interact with them. These messages accumulate to comprise the "feeling tone" or "climate" in a classroom. It is reasonable to believe that this feeling tone or climate is related to learning, feelings of esteem, acceptance, and behavior.

In short, the classroom climate and the messages we convey to children help to establish critical growth conditions in the classroom. Generally, high or positive growth conditions facilitate the development of esteem and worth while low or negative growth conditions minimize opportunities for this development. The following list characterizes teacher strategies and behaviors that constitute high and low growth conditions. While examining the list, remember that the items represent extremes on a continuum. Rarely would anyone fall completely at either end.

High Growth Conditions	Low Growth Conditions
High acceptance/respect of pupil's ideas	Low acceptance/respect of pupil's ideas
1. Pupil ideas are frequently accepted. The teacher listens to and incorporates pupil ideas in discussion and other learning situations.	1. Pupil ideas are rarely encouraged or accepted. There is little opportunity for discussion. When discussion occurs, it is highly controlled and seeks <u>recall</u> of previously learned information. Pupil contributions are frequently criticized.
High acceptance/respect of pupil's affect	Low acceptance/respect of pupil's affect
2. Pupil feelings and emotions are accepted by the teacher as long as harm to others is avoided.	2. Pupil feelings are avoided or discouraged. The teacher is unwilling to recognize expressions and discussions of feelings.
High encouragement/support of pupils	Low encouragement/support of pupils
3. Pupils are encouraged to explore, make suggestions, etc. An atmosphere of "try it and tell us what happens" pervades the classroom.	3. Pupils are discouraged from exploration. The teacher has the one right way of doing things and only that way is accepted. Alternatives are not discussed or tested.
4. The teacher is willing to "get off the subject" when an interesting event or question is raised. At times the question becomes the actual topic.	4. The teacher controls the subject at all times. Penetrating philosophical questions are discouraged. The principal aim is to teach the lesson and complete it.

High pupil individualization	Low pupil individualization
5. The teacher attempts to understand and respond to each child's psychological needs. The teacher recognizes that some children may need more direction and control while others may need the opportunity to exercise greater choice. The teacher, therefore, encourages children to learn and explore in ways that each child is comfortable with.	5. The teacher denies individual differences and needs and demands conformity. The teacher who demands that every child participate in an "open" classroom may produce the same low growth conditions as the teacher who provides a "lock-step" classroom atmosphere. Both strategies are authoritarian, and demand conformity at the possible expense of pupil feelings of esteem, control and connectedness.
High pupil involvement	Low pupil involvement
6. A continuing dialogue with pupils is maintained to involve children in making decisions about their learning (e.g., individual and small group projects, work contracts, etc.), and to help children further clarify what they are learning.	6. The teacher always tells pupils what and how they are to learn. Little room is left for pupil choice and expression.
High teacher genuiness/ realness	Low teacher genuiness/ realness
7. The teacher is genuine, willing to express ideas, feelings, experiences and be a real person rather than play a role. Where appropriate, the teacher allows students entry into his/her private world of feelings, ideas, needs, and concerns.	7. The teacher plays a role and presents a facade that conceals feelings. The teacher acts in a confined, prescribed manner revealing little of own uniqueness and inner thoughts. A wide emotional gap is maintained between teacher and pupil and little of the common bonds, needs and feelings that the two may actually possess is explored.

Essentially, high growth conditions show the willingness of the teacher to meet children at their level, to involve pupils in classroom decisions, and to maximize individualization of learning. A fundamental emphasis is on <u>listening</u> to children. Though at times all children are involved in working on the same activity, there are times when children work on individualized or self-directed activities. Rather than using authority to limit and control pupil discussion, the teacher uses authority to facilitate rational, problem-solving discussion.

This list should be considered realistically, neither too seriously nor too lightly. Even the most supportive, accepting, and sensitive teacher does not evidence high growth conditions every minute. More important is the sum total of these considerations. At the end of each day or week, can we look back and ask, "In general, did the children obtain as much as possible regarding their needs for esteem, self-understanding, and decision-making?" Can each child say, (1) "I am important here because the teacher listens to me and allows me to do some things that are important to me," (2) "I have choices here. I don't always have to do exactly what others tell me to do," and (3) "Other kids have ideas and needs. They are doing some things differently."

Merging Feeling Oriented and Fact Oriented Learning Through Discussions

Having discussed the "classroom climate," we are now ready to look at the next step, deriving feeling oriented and personal meaning from traditionally cognitive areas. We want to relate each child's learning in the knowing sense to personal feelings and values whenever possible.

To merge the affective-cognitive learning, the teacher must be aware of pupil feelings and reactions regarding what they are learning, how they are learning, why they are learning, and what is happening with their classmates while they are learning. The teacher's awareness may turn into highly productive discussion questions such as, "How would you feel or react if you were the character in this story?" "What aspects of the character's life do you see in yourself?" "How are ants' needs for social systems like ours?"

Thus, the teacher's goal is to relate academic content to pupil feelings and pupil meaning. Whenever possible, the teacher uses discussion to determine how the content relates to the feelings and values of the students. Below are some examples of how this might be done.

1. After a group activity, the class discusses the value of cooperative endeavors and sharing. Group problems may be discussed as well as the value and meaning each student derives from group work.
2. As a social studies lesson on Colonial America the teacher raises questions focusing on how the students

would feel, how their lives would be different, etc., if they were living in Colonial times.

3. After a creative rhythm (dance) activity, the class discusses the feelings the various movements evoked.
4. During reading, a story is read in which a strong emotional event occurred for one of the characters. Besides checking comprehension, the teacher asks the students how they might feel and react if they were that person.
5. During a unit on the heart, transplants are discussed. Discussion focuses on whether you are the same person if you have a new heart . . . what makes a person.
6. After new skills are learned, a discussion focuses on the meaning and value of the skills. How are you different now? What can you do now that you couldn't do before?

Such discussions are not to achieve uanimity of feelings and values. Rarely will all children derive the same feelings or meaning from a lesson. More importantly, children will have an opportunity both to discuss things they have learned cognitively and to understand the feelings and reactions the lesson evoked in themselves and others. They will have an opportunity to voice and explore their own feelings and reactions and to examine how their basic reactions, needs, and feelings are shared by other children.

Bring Feelings, Emotions, Needs, and Human Behavior Into the Curriculum

We now move away from traditional academic concerns and focus on bringing feelings and emotions, values and human behavior into the curriculum through activities that deal with the affective domain. We might:

1. develop a unit exploring basic human emotional needs and how behavior meets these needs.
2. develop a unit on roles people take (why are some people clowns, bullies, etc.)
3. develop activities to <u>help pupils gain effective group participation skills</u>.
4. conduct discussions and activities to establish more accepting and helping peer interaction.
5. develop an ongoing unit that helps each child clarify one's values, major strengths, likes, dislikes, etc.

Merging Affective and Cognitive Areas

This section focuses on improving small and large group discussions in four ways: (1) improving teacher discussion skills, (2) providing teacher techniques for maximizing pupil involvement, (3) improving pupil discussion skills and behaviors, and (4) orienting discussion to incorporate cognitive and affective objectives. Hopefully, teachers will be able to provide a classroom climate that promotes growth conditions for all pupils. This section is presented in workbook fashion. Throughout the section are practice activities for the teacher and suggested classroom activities for teachers and pupils.

Part A: Teacher behaviors that facilitate high growth conditions during class discussions - strategies for changing our own behavior.

How we "come across" to pupils during discussions is fundamental. We can respond to pupils through high growth conditions conveying messages such as, "I am interested in you," "I value your ideas," "I want to help you clarify your ideas." We can, also respond to pupils through low growth conditions conveying messages such as, "I am interested in right answers, not your ideas, reactions, etc." The relationship between growth conditions and pupil feelings of esteem and worth has already been explored. Let's now examine specific teacher discussion behaviors that help establish high growth conditions and provide for more productive class discussions whether oriented towards cognitive or feeling areas or both.

There is a critical distinction between a drill or recitation and a discussion. A drill or recitation attempts to determine what specific knowledges or skills the children have learned through reading, observing or listening. Here is an example:

Teacher: John, in what year did Richard Nixon assume the presidency?

John: Uhuh, he became president in 1966.

Teacher: No, you are close but that's wrong. Who can help you?

Sally: 1968

Teacher: Right! That's good. O.k., who was his vice president?

Notice the pattern here. A factual or information-type question was asked by the teacher. A factual answer was provided by the student involving recall of information. Finally, the teacher gave the child information or feedback as to the correctness of the response. The drill pattern is a simple question, answer, feedback; then a new question, answer, feedback. There is nothing wrong with a drill procedure when the goal is to determine whether the children have "their facts or knowledge straight." Indeed, a discussion may involve some drill sequences. However, a drill is not a discussion!

A discussion is oriented towards objectives that are more elaborate than factual recall. For example, during a specific learning activity we might use a discussion format to:
1. Examine casuality, e.g., why do you think Nixon was a popular candidate; what needs do you think motivated the boy to act the way he did?
2. Determine pupil reactions, values, feelings, e.g., how would you have reacted if you were in the situation; what would you be thinking about if you were the character in the story; how might this piece of scientific knowledge influence your life?
3. Seek solutions to problem, e.g., what could be done to prevent name-calling in our classroom; what might the character in this story have done to avoid the problem?
4. Explore consequences of actions or events (e.g., what would happen if . . .)

In short, drills involve remembering and recalling while discussion involves understanding, exploring, relating to self, speculating, projecting, evaluating, and suggesting.

Discussion allows pupils to give their own ideas, suggestions, and thoughts more frequently than drills. This emphasis on students and their ideas insures the high level growth conditions which tend to reinforce pupil self-worth and willingness to participate in discussions.

Now, let's look at five teacher behaviors and strategies that establish both higher growth conditions and higher levels of constructive pupil involvement.

1. Asking problem-solving questions: Certainly, one way to develop active, productive discussions is to raise thought provoking questions involving children in solving and exploring real or hypothetical problems. This opportunity for critical thinking may heighten pupil interest. Here are two global categories of problem-solving questions:

    A. Asking students to determine motives or causes of relationships. These open-ended "what" or "why" questions involve students in analyzing and inferring. For example, we can ask students to determine causes and/or motives ("Why do you think this happened?" "What motivates a person to act this way?" "From what you have learned, what could cause this to happen?"). We can also ask students to draw relationships between events or similarities in situations ("How are needs related to behavior?" "How is this situation like . . .(another situation)?").

B. Asking students to anticipate, suggest, or evaluate: In addition to asking students to determine causes, motives or relationships, we can ask pupils to anticipate consequences or suggest possible solutions, ("What would happen if . . .?"), ("What could solve this problem?"), and evaluate the value of certain solutions ("What would happen if we followed John's suggestions?").

Regardless of the categories, open-ended, problem-solving questions require much pupil involvement. Since we are less interested in facts (drill), pupils are likely to give multiple views and answers. These differences of opinion lead to anticipatory or evaluative questions and thought. (What do you think would happen if we did what John suggested?").

2. <u>Giving supportive pupil feedback</u>: Once a pupil has tried to answer an open-ended question, what response can we make? We can evaluate the correctness or value of the answer through praise or criticism. However, too frequent praise or criticism might orient the student to answering to please the teacher rather than giving his/her own response. A more appropriate teacher response is <u>to try to understand the pupil's answer while conveying empathy and respect for the student</u>. If the student's response is thoughtless or unclear, a clarificatory question rather than criticism can be directed towards the student. Let's examine these two types of pupil feedback.

A. Responding with empathy and respect: this response assures the pupil that his/her ideas or feelings are understood, regardless of teacher or peer agreement with the pupil's statement. We can do this by:
   (1) Rephrasing the student's response ("In other words, you are saying that . . .").
   (2) Relating the pupil's response to another student ("You seem to be agreeing with John.").
   (3) Recognizing or inferring the pupil's feelings ("It sounds as though this would make you feel very important and helpful.").
   (4) Seeking support or confirmation from other pupils ("How many other people would feel or react the way Sally did?").

   These responses help to communicate positive messages to pupils about their value and acceptance. These messages, therefore, enhance pupil esteem and feelings of worth. However, sometimes students make blatantly thoughtless or impractical suggestions. How can we stimulate more critical thinking without showing lack of acceptance or understanding? In these cases, our second preferred type of pupil feedback is the clarification question.

B. Asking clarification questions: When there is little clarity or thoughtfulness in a pupil's response, we can ask several types of clarification questions that:

(1) Seek greater clarity: We can simply ask the student to repeat or re-word a statement or give an example. We might preface this with, "I'm a little unclear about what you're saying. Could you . . ."

(2) Redirect thinking: For a thoughtless response, we might elicit greater thought by asking him/her to consider what would happen if the response were acted upon ("What do you think would happen if we acted on your suggestion?").

In summary, our response to pupil contributions may encourage or discourage further pupil participation and problem solving. Generally, when pupil contributions are met with empathy and respect, they are reinforced and encouraged. Thus, pupils come to trust the teacher and may gradually feel more willing to contribute. When pupil contributions are frequently met with praise or criticism, pupils may feel less secure about contributing.

3. Personalizing the discussion: Our third critical teacher behavior is an orienting strategy. Since pupils often have difficulty relating to abstract discussion topics which bear little relationship to their own experiences, we can personalize the discussion through questions relating the topic to the pupil's frame of reference. Questions such as "What would you do if you were in that situation?" "How would you feel . . .?" and "What would

be foremost on your mind . . .?" can personalize a
discussion, helping the class become more involved.
An example might clarify the value of this technique.
One teacher was conducting a series of problem-solving
discussions with a group of elementary children. The
topic was "What could be done if a child stole a small
sum of money from the teacher?" Numerous student
suggestions indicated a rather superficial level of
thinking. Many students quickly suggested that the
child be harshly punished ("paddle him," "expel him"
"take something away from him"). The teacher,
recognizing that the problem was perhaps too abstract,
personalized the discussion by asking, "O.k., pretend
you were that person. What would you be thinking about
and what would you want to be done?" Personalizing
the discussion by having the student place himself/
herself in the situation induced more sensitive, realistic
thinking.

4. Evaluation of the discussion: Content and process: This
strategy may, with the other three behaviors, increase
growth conditions. At various times during the discussion,
and certainly at the end, it helps to involve the pupils
in evaluating the discussion. Evaluation questions can
focus on content and meaning ("What did we learn today?"
"What is the consensus of the group?" "What was especially
meaningful to you about this discussion?"), or on process
("Last time, many people said it would help if more people

listened to what other students were saying. Did we do this today?" "What are some constructive and unconstructive things we did in today's discussion?" "Did we try to listen to each other and stay on the topic?"). Content and meaning questions focus attention on what the pupils learned or experienced through the discussion. Process oriented questions focus on how well skills of good communication (listening, giving empathic feedback, etc.) were practiced. Indeed, pupils may even make suggestions or establish guidelines for succeeding discussions.

5. Orienting the discussion: Our fifth strategy is essentially a managerial one. Since discussions (not drills) are likely to seem vague to pupils, it may help to orient the discussion. We can do this by listing or verbalizing one or two content objectives (the purpose of today's discussion is to . . .) and several process objectives (Let's try to give each other more feedback, stay on the topic, etc."). Orienting the discussion may also give the teacher a clearer sense of purpose and direction and a better understanding of when to "pull the students back to the subject" or remind them of the process objectives. Thus, orienting may occur during the discussion as well as at the beginning.

In summary, these five teacher strategies enhance pupil growth whether the discussion is academically or affectively oriented.

Let's see how these critical teacher strategies mold a discussion. The following, abbreviated discussion, demonstrates the use of four of the five critical teacher behaviors.

A Social Studies Discussion - Grade 5

1. Global objectives: (a) to help children become more aware of the hardships of early American life, (b) to help children become more aware of the similarities and differences between early American and modern life, (c) to facilitate the development of group discussion and problem-solving skills.

2. Previous experiences: (a) for two days the children have read assignments about early American life, (b) a drill or recitation activity (written and oral) of the content has already been conducted.

Teacher: "Today, let's see if we can understand some of the hardships children of your age may have faced in early American times. Let's also see if we can practice some of the good discussion skills that we talked about yesterday. Let's try to listen to each other and tell each other whether we understand, the ideas expressed. Also, let's remember to take turns (teacher lists these major points on the chalkboard)." (Teacher orients the discussion in terms of content and process objectives.)

Teacher: "You know, nowadays, it isn't too hard to get help if you are sick. What could you do if you were baby sitting for a younger brother or sister and suddenly he/she became very sick?"

(Problem-solving question - anticipate actions: Note also that the question is personalized.)

John: "Well, I'd be pretty frightened but I'd call our neighbor up right away to come over."

Teacher: "O.k., you'd be afraid and worried but you could depend on someone (teacher demonstrates empathy and respect by rephrasing the response and recognizing the feeling). What else could be done?"

Sally: "You could call the hospital or a doctor right away if you really think it's serious."

Teacher: "O.k., from what Sally and John said, we really do have some choices. We can call a neighbor, a doctor, or a hospital. An ambulance could even be at your house in five minutes (teacher demonstrates empathy and respect again by rephrasing)."

Teacher: "Well, this is the year 1973. Suppose it were the year 1720 and you faced the same situation? What could you do?" (Teacher asks problem-solving question - anticipates actions - and personalizes the question.)

Tom: "Well, like John, I'd call a neighbor."

Teacher: "You'd call for help (teacher demonstrates empathy and respect by rephrasing) but what would your chances of getting help be?"

(Teacher redirects pupil's thinking to more careful thought.)

Tom: "Well, I still think someone would be around."

Teacher: "O.k., you would count on someone being nearby to help you out (respect and empathy by rephrasing). What do some other people think about Tom's idea (teacher asks problem-solving question - evaluation of an idea or action)?"

Sue: "I'm not sure. I really doubt if people would be nearby and there weren't telephones in those days. I think I'd be scared to death!"

Jerry: "That goes for me, too. You probably couldn't even get a doctor."

Teacher: "That spells trouble, doesn't it? Sally and Jerry don't see much hope and Sue would be really scared because she knows her sister or brother badly needs medical attention but she can't do anything (teacher demonstrates respect and empathy by rephrasing the contributions and recognizing Sue's feelings). How many other people might feel like Sue - frightened and powerless?" (Teacher responds further with empathy by seeking confirmation from other students regarding Sue's feelings.)

This teacher frequently utilizes the critical behaviors. She opens the discussion by establishing both content and process objectives; frequently asks broad, problem-solving type questions; gives supportive feedback conveying empathy and respect; and personalizes the entire tone of the discussion. The only behavior missing is encouraging pupil evaluation of the content and meaning later or during the discussion.

Translating Ideas Into Actions:
Self-Teaching Activities

Applying newly learned techniques takes practice. This section lists a number of self-teaching activities to help you apply discussion strategies in your classroom. Remember that change does not usually occur overnight. Just as you will have to get used to the strategies, so will the children need time and practice to adjust. It might help to expect small changes in the behavior of yourself and your children over a period of weeks or months. Examine the various self-teacher strategies, feeling free to use any or all of them, or to create your own, so that you systematically begin working toward translating ideas into actions.

Activity #1: Where am I--What are my goals?

Directions: Our ability to accept divergent pupil responses during discussion is just as important as the five discussion strategies. Can we assume a less-judgmental and more accepting/supporting strategy with the children? Pretend you could detach yourself and observe yourself as a teacher, and complete the following questionnaire:

		Very Little	Somewhat	Very Much
1.	The teacher takes time to answer pupil questions	1	2	3
2.	The teacher conducts discussions (vs. drills)	1	2	3
3.	The teacher conveys empathy and respect to pupils	1	2	3

		Very Little	Somewhat	Very Much
4.	The teacher asks broad problem-solving questions during discussions	1	2	3
5.	The teacher does not get too upset when pupils make thoughtless suggestions	1	2	3
6.	When pupils make thoughtless suggestions, the teacher helps them reconsider their comments	1	2	3
7.	The teacher frequently criticizes pupils	1	2	3
8.	The teacher seems concerned not only about correct answers but also about the pupils' feelings, reasons, etc.	1	2	3
9.	There is a "give and take" spirit between the teacher and pupils	1	2	3
10.	The teacher is willing to "get off the topic" to discuss specific pupil questions	1	2	3

"How did I do?" List the areas in which this teacher needs to improve.

1. _____
2. _____
3. _____
4. _____

A Contract: Write a contract for yourself regarding your discussion behavior. Use any or all of the following activities to help you fulfill the contract.

1. I wish to improve my performance or skills in the following five (5) teacher-discussion strategies (list the behaviors you wish to improve; you may choose all five (5) or only those most relevant).

A. _____
B. _____

C. _____

D. _____

E. _____

2. Now, look over the suggested activities and write down those you plan to complete to accomplish your contract. I will engage in the following activities:

   # _____   # _____   # _____   # _____

Activity #2: Imagine

Take ten minutes and practice a classroom discussion in your own mind incorporating the five critical discussion strategies. Use the following guide:

1. Step one: Think of a discussion topic for your class relating to a current learning activity. Think of both knowing and feeling objectives. Pretend you are writing these objectives on the chalkboard to orient the students to content and process objectives.

    A. List some content objectives that focus on knowing and feeling: the purpose of today's discussion is to . . .
    _____
    _____

    B. List some process objectives that structure or call for particular types of student participation or thinking: remember during the discussion, try to . . . _____
    _____

2. Step two: List several open-ended problem-solving questions that focus on understanding motives or causes ("why" type questions) and on suggesting actions, anticipating consequences, etc. Personalize these questions to relate to the students' frame of reference. The questions should relate to your knowing and feeling objectives.

    A. _____
    B. _____
    C. _____

D. _____

E. _____

3. Step three: Imagine a response from a pupil. The pupil tells how he/she would feel and what he/she would do in a certain situation. Write down the _feedback_ you would give to the student to demonstrate your empathy and respect.

_____

_____

_____

Imagine another pupil; a silly unconstructive suggestion is given. Some older children chuckle. Instead of criticizing the pupil, demonstrate empathy and respect by asking a follow-up question that gets the child to reconsider his contribution.

_____

_____

_____

Imagine another pupil; the pupil says something that demonstrates a great deal of conviction and strong feelings. The student is almost crying. Respond with empathy and respect, showing that you recognize the child's feelings.

_____

_____

_____

Try to elicit support from other pupils regarding the child's feelings by asking:

_____

_____

_____

4. Step four: Think about questions involving the students in evaluating the content process aspects of the discussion. Have the group set some process objectives for the next discussion.

_____

_____

_____

Activity #3: Practice in your classroom by conducting several discussions

Take your list of discussion behaviors and practice these strategies in a series of small group discussions with your students. You may want to practice in groups that are already formed. Before beginning, establish goals for yourself; e.g., "I want to involve pupils in examining motivation behind the behavior of the characters in the story," "I want to respond to each pupil's contribution with empathy and respect by rephrasing, recognizing feelings, etc." Set up a score sheet for yourself (see sample score sheet) with the critical behaviors. As you demonstrate each behavior give yourself a checkmark, or tape record the discussion and check your behavior later. Conduct these practice sessions several times until you feel comfortable with the behaviors.

Sample Score Sheet and Guide Sheet

Date _____ Activity _____ Time _____

1. My objectives for this lesson are to practice the following behaviors:

   _____
   _____

2. How often I demonstrated each behavior (place a checkmark along side the behavior each time you demonstrate it).

   A. Asking open-ended questions_____

   B. Feedback that demonstrates empathy and respect_____

   C. Personalizing a question_____

D. Orienting the discussion_____

E. Evaluating the discussion_____

Activity #4: Practicing in large group class discussions

In your class discussions, list goals for yourself as in Activity #3. Conduct the discussion checking each goal behavior as you demonstrate it. If the children ask what you are doing, tell them you are trying to change your behavior. Do this for several discussions.

Activity #5: Elicit help from the children or a colleague

At the beginning tell them your goals . Ask them how they think you did at the end. Invite a colleague to observe you. Tell him/her what you are trying to do before beginning. Have your colleague or one or two of your students "keep score" using the checkmark system.

Activity #6: Conduct an experiment with your pupils

Ask your pupils to help determine what kind of adult or teacher behaviors they like best. First, conduct a five or ten minute discussion attempting to demonstrate all five of the critical discussion strategies. When the time period is up, pass out the "Pupil Evaluation Form" for each student to complete immediately. Then conduct another discussion demonstrating the opposite or negative teacher behaviors. Again have the pupils complete a new copy of the "Pupil Evaluation Form". Then have the pupils summarize the scores for each item by setting up a frequency distribution (see the example). Find out how the class as a whole felt during the first discussion and compare the results

with the second discussion. Discuss with the children what a good
discussion involves, how the teacher can make the pupil feel, etc.
CAUTION! To make sure the pupils understand that this is an
experiment, tell them you will demonstrate two different ways of
discussing. Remind them that this is a "pretend" activity.

Pupil Evaluation Form

Circle the answer that tells how much you agree with the statement.

		Strongly Agree	Agree A Little	Disagree
1.	I felt comfortable in the discussion	3	2	1
2.	The teacher listened carefully to the students	3	2	1
3.	I wanted to participate in the discussion	3	2	1
4.	The teacher showed that she really liked and respected students in the classroom	3	2	1
5.	_____ (Add your own item)	3	2	1
6.	_____ (Add your own item)	3	2	1

7. If this kind of person were my teacher every day, I would feel

Scoring Procedures - Frequency Distribution

First Discussion	Number of Children Who Responded in Each Category		
	Strongly Agree	Agree A Little	Disagree
1. I felt comfortable in the discussion	3	2	1
2. The teacher listened carefully to the students	3	2	1
3. I wanted to participate in the discussion	3	2	1
4. The teacher showed that she really liked and respected students in the discussion	3	2	1
5. _____	3	2	1
6. _____	3	2	1

7. If this kind of person were my teacher every day, I would feel

Repeat the tally for the second discussion.

Part B: Techniques to increase pupil involvement and participation in discussion.

Most of us think of school discussions as directly involving the teacher, leading the entire class at the same time. These large group or entire class discussions frequently have certain liabilities. Typically, only several pupils consistently participate. Less involved students play only a passive role. This section describes other discussion techniques to be used to fortify the large group approach and increase pupil participation. There are: (1) mini-group techniques; (2) case analysis procedures; (3) buzz groups; and (4) dyadic or two-person interchanges. Although these techniques overlap in form and purpose, they will be individually discussed.

1. Large group techniques: Little need be said about this approach since we are most familiar with it. Obviously the 5 discussion techniques apply to large group discussions. Arranging pupils in a circle, or so they can see each other, will enhance communication and increase participation.

    The large group technique can be used for giving directions, raising problems, summarizing pupil ideas, and further discussion. Pupils may then be organized into any one of the following arrangements to focus on discussion issues.

2. Mini groups: Perhaps the most direct way to increase pupil involvement and participation is to break the class into smaller or "mini" discussion groups. Pupils should be given clear discussion topics and be reminded

of particular skills and behaviors to practice. Discussion leaders may be appointed or may simply emerge. The teacher can "roam" among the various groups as a resource person. At the end of a specified time the groups can reform into a large group for reporting and summarizing.

3. Buzz groups: Buzz groups, a varient of mini groups, are smaller with no more than five or six to a group and are shorter in their duration. This is an excellent way to get preliminary ideas, opinions, and feedback regarding a particular topic or problem. These ideas or opinions may then be discussed by the entire class, or in mini-groups. Another type is "brainstorming groups". They are also buzz groups, which are assigned to come up with preliminary suggestions to be further discussed in a large group.

4. Case example or situation analysis: As in large or small groups, students are given a written account of a particular situation or series of events which may involve literary, historical, or political characters. Pupils then analyze or discuss specific aspects of the case or situation. After a specified time the groups present their suggestions in a large group, where feedback and further discussion may occur. Here are three sample cases to be analyzed.

   A. Sally is a lonely third grader. Nobody in class gives her any attention. Some kids even make fun of her because she comes to school in old, dirty clothes. Sally is also not very good in math or reading. Some kids call her dumb, ugly, or stupid. Sally sometimes goes home and cries by herself because she is so unhappy. Suppose Sally were in your class. What things could help Sally feel better? Would you help Sally? How?

B. The adoption of the Declaration of Independence was, in fact, not popular with all Americans. However, it was signed and most of the American people adopted its resolutions. Did we have any justification for not obeying English laws and governors? Was our gain worth the loss of so many lives? What were some conditions leading to the decisions to become an independent nation?

C. Our system of government has two major political parties. What would be advantages or disadvantages of having four or five major parties, or of having only one party.

5. <u>Dyadic interactions</u>: Students may break into pairs to discuss specific topics or issues. This technique may be particularly useful for very shy and timid students. Dyadic interchanges have many other possible uses. For example:

    A. One student can interview another student to determine that student's ideas and perceptions.
    B. Pairs of students who disagree on a topic may informally "debate" an issue.
    C. Problem-solving tasks may be tackled in pairs.

D. Personal or interpersonal conflicts may be discussed
in pairs.

Each of the group techniques can usually be used very flexibly.
Discussions may frequently begin and end as large group discussions.
However, the various work groups (mini groups, buzz groups, case
analysis groups, and dyads) may be used in between to facilitate
higher levels of pupil involvement and participation in discussions
that are not teacher-led. It will be important, particularly the
first few times, to carefully structure the discussion questions
or topics.

Part C: Enhancing specific pupil discussion skills

We have examined ways that the classroom teacher can enhance
Level I conditions in discussion groups. Five important discussion
and group organization strategies were presented. While improving
our facility with these strategies we can also help the children
enhance their discussion skills through several simple and direct
procedures. These are similar to the self-instructional procedures
you may be using to improve your own discussion behaviors. Let's
examine some pupil objectives and then some skill development
exercises to improve pupil discussion.

Some pupil discussion skills to increase

This partial list shows important and easily observed pupil
discussion skills. You may wish to add or delete items from this
list.

1. Listening to other pupils: It is hard to tell when students
are listening. One fairly clear way to tell if a pupil has

been listening is if the speaker alludes to, summarizes, or partially paraphrases what a previous pupil said. Listening, a critical skills in any communication, is particularly important in discussions. Demonstrating that one has "listened to" a previous speaker shows support and acceptance of that speaker. Good listening also helps keep pupils focusing on the discussion and exploring ideas with greater depth and precision.

2. Asking other students questions: It helps for students to begin asking fellow students problem-solving questions, particularly in small group discussions. Here are several global types of questions:

    A. "Why" type questions that focus on understanding, meaning, and giving reasons.

    B. "What if" type questions that focus on anticipating outcomes and speculating.

    C. "What would you do/how would you feel" type questions that ask students to put themselves in a situation and anticipate how they would feel or what they would do.

3. Giving feedback: Just as a teacher can give feedback so can pupils, a helpful skill both in large and small group discussions. We can specify at least two forms of giving feedback:

    A. Showing agreement, understanding, or support of another pupil's contribution.

    B. Showing disagreement.

    Severe criticism, making fun of an unthoughtful contribution, and other such reactions should be specified as unhelpful

responses and avoided. For some children it might help to
have them substitute severe criticism with a follow-up
question to help the student consider the value or outcome
of a response. This is similar to the teacher asking a
follow-up question to redirect thinking.

Some pupil discussion behaviors to decrease

While listening, asking questions, and giving feedback are
desirable behaviors to increase, sometimes you might want to
decrease certain behaviors. Here are some troublesome group
behaviors:

1. Interrupting speakers: Some children have difficulty taking turns and may frequently interrupt, "blurting out" their comments while another pupil is talking.
2. Monopolizing the discussion: Some pupils simply over contribute reducing the opportunities for their peers to actively take part. The monopolizing pupil may also cause frustration to other children.

Thus, there are at least five behaviors for pupils to work
on. Of these behaviors summarized in Table 3, three are behaviors
to increase and two are behaviors to decrease during small or
large group discussions. You may wish to add or delete other
behaviors.

TABLE 3

Some Critical Pupil Discussion Behavior

Behaviors to Increase

1. Listening: The pupil demonstrates listening by alluding, repeating, or paraphrasing the contribution of a previous speaker before making another statement or asking a question.
2. Directing problem-solving questions to other pupils: The pupil directs a problem-solving question to another pupil.
3. Giving feedback: The pupil conveys agreement, acceptance, understanding, or disagreement with the contribution of a previous student.

Behaviors to Decrease

4. Interrupting speakers: Instead of speaking while another pupil is talking, wait until you are recognized.
5. Monopolizing: Instead of trying to answer every question, give other pupils a chance to talk.

Activities to Enhance Pupil Discussion Skills

Below is a list of skill development activities to help children improve the five pupil discussion skills. Look these over and use or modify those that seem most relevant.

Activity #1: Listening and repeating verbatim

Organize your class into one or two circles with the students sitting as close to each other as possible. Whisper into the ear of a student a three, four, or five word phrase. Tell the student to pass the message on exactly as it was whispered to him/her. When the message finally gets to the last person, have him/her state the message out loud. Check to see if the exact words were repeated. Do this with several different messages, letting the students select messages. At the end, conduct a brief discussion about the importance of listening. You may even use this activity as a "warm up" in your reading groups.

Activity #2: Listening and repeating in a discussion

Initiate this activity in small or large ongoing discussion groups such as reading, social studies, etc. Establish a ground rule that no one, including you, can talk until he/she first repeats what the previous speaker said. You may use this for several discussions to orient the children to listening more carefully. Go over progress and problems with the pupils at the end of each discussion.

Activity #3: Giving feedback

As before, a ground rule is established, being that no one

may talk until first giving feedback to the previous speaker.
Indeed, activities 2 and 3 can be combined so that pupils must
repeat, give feedback and then make their own contributions.

Activity #4: Building listening and question asking skills:
The Interview

Divide the class into pairs. Assign one child in each pair
to be the interviewer and the second person to be the interviewee.
Give the interviewers an assignment such as:

1. "Find out as much important information as you can; e.g.
   birthdate, favorite activities, etc., about the interviewee."
2. "Find out what was this person's happiest day, saddest
   day, or most frightening experience, etc."

Remind the interviewers to get as many facts and details as possible
by asking questions. At the end of a five minute time limit, have
the reporters give a brief summary or report about their interviewee
(this will orient the interviewers to careful listening). Repeat
this activity on various occasions using different topics, even
allowing the children to interview parents, community members, and
other children regarding specific issues.

Activity #5: Mini discussions

Organize the class into groups of 6, 8, or 10, sitting in
circles on the floor. Give each group a provocative discussion
topic such as the following or a topic related to a unit that is
underway.

1. Suppose all schools were closed down because there was
   no more money to run them. Would you be able to learn
   anything? What would you learn and how would you learn?

2. Suppose everyone in this group were the most important leaders in the country and you had a chance to make new laws and change the country. What would you want to change?

3. Suppose there were a blind boy in this class. How do you think the child would feel? What special things would he need? What would you do to help him feel a part of the class?

Before starting any discussion distribute and review with the children a list of the five critical discussion behaviors presented on page 36. Ask them to follow the suggestions as carefully as possible during the mini discussion having each child to record his/her contributions and discussion performance. Each time a child rephrases, demonstrating listening skills, an "x" or a checkmark is entered under the section on the list that says "Listening." Allow the groups ten minutes for discussion. Repeat the mini discussion, using a different topic, over several days. At the beginning of each mini discussion, encourage the children to improve their performances for critical behavior.

Activity #6: A training game using mini discussions

To convert Activity #5 into a highly motivating game format, assign each critical behavior a point value (i.e., listening = 1 point; asking a question = 2 points; giving feedback = 3 points; interrupting = -2 points). Divide the class into groups of five, one group sitting in an inner-circle with another group in an outer circle. The inner group contains the "players" and the outer has "observers." Each observer is to observe the player seated in front of him/her during a 7-8 minute discussion. As in Activity #5 each observer observes the "partner" and keeps a record of the partner's contributions. To avoid monopolizing, each player can talk only five different times. At the end of the discussion, the players "pool" all of their points for a group total. Then the observers and players switch roles for another discussion.

Since winners can be determined several ways, competition between groups can be introduced daily by declaring the group with the most points the winner. Competition can be decreased by totaling the points for the entire class. The class would "win" if it's total was higher the next day than on the previous day. Naturally, other varieties regarding scoring and winning can be introduced.

It may take several sessions to insure accurate observers and scorers. Remind the observers that it is possible to "chain" behaviors. A player may demonstrate listening and then ask a question. In this case, the player, using only one of his talking opportunities, has earned two checkmarks - one worth 2 points and the other worth 3 points. A "Grand Slam" would occur if the student repeats, gives feedback, and then asks a question! Interruptions, scored only as interruptions, do not receive any positive credit.

Part D: Merging feeling oriented learning and knowledge oriented learning through group discussions. (Level II concerns)

The basic goal of Level II concerns is the pursuit of cognitive objectives and feeling/meaning objectives simultaneously.

Critical in merging affective and cognitive learning is to recognize that pupils may have concerns and feelings about what they are learning, how they are learning, why they are learning, the relationship between themselves and others, etc. The most basic Level II concerns involve an awareness that the following affectively oriented issues can be merged with traditional academics:

1. How does each academic subject relate to the daily lives of the children?
2. What emotional needs, values, beliefs, and desires are expressed by people in other cultures or by story characters?
3. How do the needs, conflicts, and values of the people of other cultures or story characters relate to the needs, conflicts, and values of children?
4. How do students perceive the meaning and value of what and how they are learning?

Thus, along with mastery of knowledge, children can explore human behavior, values, and needs and how these relate to their own experiences, values, and needs. With this awareness, the teacher may structure discussions and activities so that both cognitive and affective objectives are jointly pursued.

The following demonstrates how, through questions, teachers can orient pupils to affective aspects of everyday cognitive learning activities. At other times, a specific time may be solely devoted to cognitive or affective aspects. The key to Level II discussions is the teacher's willingness and ability to structure questions that focus children on the "human" aspects of various subjects.

Example #1: After reading a story about a prisoner, the class may form a large group discussion. Questions might include some of the following:
1. "How might you feel if you were sentenced to life in prison?" (Personalizing the discussion)
2. "What might have been some reasons for the prisoner's decision to resort to crime?" (Asking students to determine motives or causes)
3. "What needs common to most people were suggested in the story? Have you experienced any of these needs? (Connectedness)
4. "How might the circumstances leading to the crime be eliminated?" (Asking students to evaluate and make suggestions)

Example #2: After a group, the teacher may have the class discuss not only the result of their efforts but also some of the interactions, feelings, problems and advantages of groups. Example discussion questions:
1. "What are the advantages of groups not found in individual activity?" (Asking for evaluation)

Example #3: During a lesson on primitive cultures, the teacher might ask questions to explore a number of affective concerns.
1. "What values held by the people in this primitive culture are similar to some in our own culture? Relate your personal values to those of the culture." (Connectedness)

2. "How do you think you might feel living under the conditions of the tribesmen?" (Personalizing the discussion)
3. "What basic needs do all men have regardless of their culture?" (Connectedness)
4. "What would happen if the tribesmen were suddenly moved to a large city to live?" (Asking for anticipation of consequences)

Example #4: After playing various pieces of classical music, the students might discuss, in a large group, the effects that the music had on their feelings.

1. "How did you feel when the classical music by Bach was playing (Personalizing the discussion)
2. "What are some benefits of music?" (Asking for evaluation)

Example #5: During an ecology lesson, the teacher might stimulate student expressions of thoughts and feelings.

1. "What feelings do you have about our responsibility to preserve wild life on our earth?" (Personalizing the discussion)
2. "Why do people 'enjoy' hunting animals?" (Asking for motives)
3. "What do you experience when you see polluted rivers, dead animals, or destroyed forests?" (Personalizing the discussion)
4. "What can we do to help reverse ecological suicide?" (Asking for suggestions)

Example #6: After a mathematics lesson, the teacher might allow time for some group discussion.

1. "What benefit might the math you learned today have for
   you today or in the future?" (Asking for suggestions
   or anticipation)
2. "How do you feel about learning new mathematical concepts?"
   (Personalizing the discussion)

Example #7: After a history lesson about the role of athletic contests in the Greek culture, allow some large group discussion time.

1. "What value or harm is there in competitive activities?"
   (Asking for evaluation or suggestion)
2. "From your personal experience, what kinds of feelings
   are aroused during competition?" (Personalizing the
   discussion)
3. "What are some advantages of team as opposed to individual
   games?" (Asking for evaluation)

Affective and Cognitive Intergration Summary

The examples, hopefully, show that cognitive (academic) objectives and affective (feeling) objectives may be accomplished simultaneously, with each aspect of learning enhancing the development of the other.

Obviously, the affective and cognitive domains of learning can and should complement each other in the classroom.

The Use of Critical Discussion Strategies & Discussion Technique: A Summary

The previous examples of affective and cognitive integration show how critical teacher strategies may be applied to seek active

student involvement through discussion. These examples have
included questions that seek motives, causes, relationships,
anticipation, suggestions, evaluation, and personalization of
the discussion. Other critical discussion strategies within
the large group format are feedback, clarifactory comments,
and discussion evaluation questions.

Although these examples focus on the large group format,
other discussion formats are presented in the section on Discussion
Technique. Try to become familiar with the potential values and
relationships of each discussion format.

Activities to Bring the Affective
Domain into the Classroom

Introduction

We have examined some critical discussion behaviors central to affective education. We focused on teacher behaviors critical in establishing a healthy, growth-enhancing classroom climate regardless of learning goals. We can approach students in ways that enhance pupil esteem and feelings of worth. We then focused on critical teacher and pupil class discussion behaviors which merge affective needs with cognitive goals.

Now we are concerned with deliberate efforts to bring human behavior into the everyday curriculum through planned activities and units. An example would be an ongoing unit on affective education focusing on:

1. Understanding basic emotional needs.
2. Observing and discussing behaviors used to meet needs.
3. Exploring how we can satisfy or frustrate needs of others.
4. Examining ways we behave and the impact of this behavior on the needs and feelings of our peers.
5. Dealing with feelings of anger, frustration, and hostility.
6. Developing constructive interpersonal skills such as helping and cooperating.
7. Developing strategies for resolving peer conflicts.
8. Clarifying personal needs and examining specific mastery skills such as competence, self-control, and interpersonal skills.

This brief list of goals can be expanded and made specific to focus on daily lessons involving readings, discussion, and various small and large group activities.

Part A: Tools and Techniques

It is difficult to summarize all of the affective activities or to accurately list the general types of affective tools. However, for this manual three broad types of tools will be presented: (1) small group activities focusing on developing interpersonal skills and understandings; (2) paper and pencil self-exploration activities; and (3) group discussion activities focusing on understanding needs, behavior, and feelings. Any classroom unit or lesson could involve these affective activities. Read over the techniques to get an idea of both methods and objectives of Level III concerns.

1. Small Group Activities and Games to Develop Interpersonal Skills and Sensitivities:

The following activities and games have many purposes and objectives. Among these objectives would be to provide structured experiences that:

    A. Allow students to explore and practice specific helping skills.

    B. Help students develop awareness of, and sensitivity to, their own feelings and the feelings of their peers.

    C. Encourage students to discuss and consider human feelings and needs.

D. Let students practice "playing" a variety of roles and experience verbal and non-verbal forms of communication.

E. Foster group cohesion and a spirit of co-operation through enjoying creative group activities.

In addition, most of the activities are fun. Since they primarily involve creative movement and expression, children who have difficulties in reading will not be handicapped in their participation. Hopefully, you and your children will be able to generate many variations and new activities to supplement the examples here.

1.1 Warm-Ups--Pantomining Events, Actions, and Feelings

I. Objectives

A. To give students "warm-up" activities to gradually familiarize them with role-playing, non-verbal communication, and creative group interactions.

B. To give students an opportunity to practice participation and cooperation through pantomine skills.

C. To sensitize pupils to expressive, non-verbal communication.

D. To give students an initial opportunity to explore human feelings.

II. Methods

A. Set A: Pantomining basic actions and events. Pupils are organized into one large or several small groups. Each person is to non-verbally pantomine or role play while the other members try to guess what the child is attempting to convey. Tasks may include pantomining: (1) your favorite activity; (2) an important thing you did over the weekend; (3) something you like to do; (4) your favorite animal; or (5) things other people do.

B. Set B: Encouraging cooperation through pantomine. After the pupils have developed some basic pantomine or role playing skills, have them present skits in pairs or small groups. At first you may assign topics such as "playing catch" "eating lunch," "playing cards," " "watching a basketball game," "being a forest showing the growth of trees through the seasons," or "a marching band." Later, students may design their own skits. Have the watching students see if they can determine what the skit depicted.

C. Set C: Pantomining feelings. Organize pupils into pairs or small groups, and provide each with a set of feeling cards (3 x 5 cards) with a feeling written on each card (i.e., love, anger, fear, surprise, pain, sadness, embarrassment, shock, worry, excitement, or uncertainty). One person picks a card and pantomines the feelings, using eyes, mouth, hands, and facial expression but no words. The partner has to guess the feeling. Later, after demonstrating an emotion, the person might recall a personal experience that actually elicited such an emotion.

III. <u>Discussion/Follow-up</u>

These activities may serve as a "warm-up" for several weeks, or may be used as "ice-breakers" at the beginning of other discussion activities. After each warm-up activity, allow the pupils to share their reactions and to evaluate the session in terms of how they felt, what they learned about pantomine, role playing, communication, or the problems and joys of working together.

1.2 Mirroring

I. Objectives

    A. To allow students to express their thoughts and feelings non-verbally.

    B. To allow students to interact and reflect the non-verbal behaviors or feelings of someone else.

    C. To allow students to receive non-verbal feedback from someone else about previous physical behaviors or expressions of feelings.

II. Methods

Divide the students into dyads. One member of each dyad is called a "person" and the other is called a "mirror." The "mirror" is to mimic or reflect everything the "person" does.

Have the members of each dyad stand facing each other. The "person" might begin by making large movements of the body, arms, legs, and head. The "mirror" reflects what his partner does. Later, facial expressions and various feelings may be made and reflected. After a few minutes, reverse roles.

III. Discussion/Follow-up

After dyad members have played both roles, have a discussion considering some of the following points:

A. As the "person," did you have any difficulty thinking of things to do or express?
B. What were some difficult feelings to express non-verbally?
C. As the "mirror," what problems did you have in mirroring the "person"?
D. When you viewed your reflection, did you see something about your actions or expressions that you had not seen before? What?
E. Did the activity help you to know each other better? Explain.

Time may be allowed for discussion between the pairs, followed by a large group discussion.

As a follow-up, students may use the previous technique to express feelings, needs, wishes, bodily and rhythmic movements, etc. The activity may be an ongoing attempt to gain greater understanding of each other.

1.3 Blind Journey

I. Objectives

A. To allow students to experience some problems of blind people.
B. To allow students to practice helping others.
C. To allow students to be dependent upon someone and to be responsible for someone's safety and welfare.

D. To discuss how we can influence other people's feelings of trust and safety.

II. Method

After students are paired, one student in each pair is blindfolded. The non-blindfolded partner leads the blindfolded person around for five minutes being as helpful and reassuring as possible. Roles are then reversed for another "tour."

III. Discussion/Follow-up

After the activity, discussion might focus on these questions: (1) what did it feel like to be blind, (2) what were you most worried about when blindfolded, (3) what things about trusting others have you learned, (4) how did it feel to be responsible for someone's safety, (5) what did you learn about blind people, and (6) did you trust your safety to your sighted partner? Why? Why not? The discussion may start in dyads and then moved to a large group.

Follow-up activities might include (1) expanding the time while blindfolded, (2) having partners feed each other, (3) participating in a class while "blind," (4) teaching a blind partner several reading or "sight vocabulary words" through a tactile or kinesthetic procedure (i.e., use sand paper letters). Conduct a discussion after each of these activities.

1.4 "Seeing" Without Our Eyes

I. Objectives

A. To improve the accuracy of giving and following directions.

B. To improve verbal expression.

C. To enhance sensitivity to kinesthetic stimuli.

D. To enhance pupil sharing and cooperation.

II. Method

A. Set A: Put several different objects into a box or bag. A blindfolded student reaches into the bag or box, selects an object and tries to identify it by feel, smell, sound, or even taste.

B. Set B: Each member of a pair develops a "grab bag" containing several objects. After blindfolding one member, the sighted member directs his partner to select specific items. Allow the children to place more items in the bag the second time they try the activity.

C. Set C: Treasure hunt. The sighted partner of a pair of children hides an object somewhere in the classroom. From a stationary position, the sighted partner must direct the blindfolded partner to the treasure.

III. Discussion/Follow-up

After each activity, discuss the problems and insights the students obtained through a sensory modality, the problems and significance of giving clear and precise details, and how they felt and what they learned.

1.5 Jungle Symphony

I. Objectives
   A. To let students cooperate to create a large group product.
   B. To allow students to practice listening and following directions.
   C. To allow students to engage in a creative and expressive non-verbal activity.
   D. To build a spirit of close cooperation among the students and to see the benefits of large group cooperation and helping.

II. Method
   A. Obtain a tape recorder and seat the children on the floor.
   B. Briefly discuss what a symphony is (i.e., there are many different instruments and the players are under the leadership of a conductor or the teacher).
   C. Tell the students that they are going to create a symphony without instruments--a Jungle Symphony. Here are the steps involved:
      1. Obtain players: Ask the students what animals live in the jungle. As a pupil suggests an animal,(e.g., "a lion") ask the pupil to make that animal's sound. Find others wishing to be that animal and sit them together. Repeat this until you have 5 or 6 animal sections such as birds, monkeys, snakes, elephants, even a tarzan or hunter. Some of the students may giggle at first but do not discourage them.

2. Practice: Once the players are in their sections conduct a brief practice. As the conductor, you will give them 3 signals (you may think of more signals):
   a. Raise your hand--section become louder
   b. Lower your hand--section becomes softer
   c. Point--section begins their sound. (Have each section practice following your signal.)
3. Conduct the symphony: Place the tape recorder in the center of the symphony to record it. Think of a sequence of sounds that will make a story (i.e., the animals are gathered at a watering hole and are frightened away by the lions or a hunter). Play out the story by directing the sections.

III. Discussion/Follow-up

Play back the symphony, asking the students to determine the story. Discuss how the pupils felt while making and listening to the symphony. Ask them what would have happened if the groups had not cooperated.

As a follow-up, have the children draw pictures of their symphony, or make up stories and act as conductors in larger or smaller groups. Construct different symphonies (i.e., "sounds of the city," "country evening," etc.) Record each symphony for the children to listen to at their leisure.

1.6 Group Puzzle Activity

I. Objectives

A. To allow students to solve a problem requiring non-verbal cooperation.

B. To allow students to examine their approach to cooperative activities.

C. To allow students to follow directions in a motor activity.

II. Method

Using construction paper, cut out four or five sets of large puzzles having the following pieces:

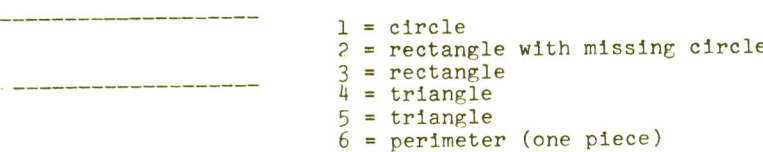

```
1 = circle
2 = rectangle with missing circle
3 = rectangle
4 = triangle
5 = triangle
6 = perimeter (one piece)
```

The puzzle contains 6 pieces as indicated. Randomly pass out one piece to each pupil. Since 4 puzzles will have 24 pieces and 5 puzzles will have 30 pieces, only multiples of 6 can play (18, 24, 30, or 36). Appoint "extra" children as observers. Write on the chalkboard the pieces needed to make a puzzle (i.e., one circle, one rectangle with missing circle, etc.). Instruct the children that this is a game of cooperating or helping each other and they are to find other children to complete a puzzle. Stop when all the children have found groups of six and completed the puzzle. The only ground rule is that the children must solve the problem non-verbally by walking about the room.

III. Discussion/Follow-up

When all the children have solved the puzzle, have them remain in their groups of six. Discuss the following questions with the class:

A. How did each group solve the problem? Was there a leader? How did the leader behave?

B. How did people treat each other?

C. How did you feel, not being able to talk?

D. What did you learn about yourself and how you behave when you need something from someone else? Do you fulfill that need by considering the needs and feelings of others?

E. How is this activity like living in a family, a classroom, at work, or being on a team?

To follow up repeat the activity using more or less complex puzzles, or have the students make up puzzles. Discuss the advantages of cooperation as well as ways that people can behave in groups that are considerate of others' needs and feelings.

1.7 Interviewer

I. Objectives

A. To have students practice listening, question-asking, and report skills.

B. To have students share important experiences with each other.

II. Method

After grouping into pairs, one student interviews the other student for a newspaper report. The interviewee focuses on "the happiest moment of my life." The interviewer must ask questions finding out as many details as possible. At the end of (5-10 minutes), let students reverse role. After

the interviews, each interviewer gives a report about the
interviewee to a small group or to the entire class.

III. Discussion/Follow-up

After each "report" the teacher asks the interviewee if
the details were presented properly. A discussion then focuses
on good interviewing behavior with a list of good interviewing
techniques drawn up and recorded for later use with topics
switching to "the worst thing that ever happened to me," etc.
Try to determine if interview behaviors improve with practice.
A number of variations can be conducted, for example, pupils
can interview adults, construct surveys, and engage in a
variety of "data collection" procedures.

1.8 Counselor

I. Objectives

A. To allow students to help another pupil to solve a problem.
B. To practice exploring feelings, defining problems, defining alternatives, and selecting strategies.

II. Method

Assign one member of a pair the role of "counselor/helper"
and the other pupil the role "student with a problem." Select
one problem for all students (e.g., "A kid in class keeps
picking on me, by always pushing me around, making me give
answers, and threatening to hurt me if I don't do his/her work.
What can I do?"). Counselors are to help the pupil solve the
problem. Before beginning, meet with the "counselors" and
"problem students" separately. Tell the counselors not to

give advice but to determine both the problem and how the pupil feels. The counselor should help the pupil select a strategy. The teacher should meet with the pupils to make sure they understand what their problem is, and allow the pairs 10 minutes for counseling.

III. Discussion/Follow-up

Assemble the entire group and allow each "counselor" to discuss his/her "case." Also, allow the "student" to mention how his/her counselor helped. Discuss the difficulties of being a counselor, good counseling techniques, how the counselor can make the pupil feel good or bad, etc. Repeat the activity several times using different problems. Reverse roles so each student has a chance to be the "counselor." Follow-up activities can cover many problem situations involving pupils in problem-solving and sensitize the pupils to the problems of other people. For example:

A. A teacher has a student whose behavior the teacher cannot manage. The principal must counsel the teacher.

B. A student is frequently called names by classmates. The counselor must listen to the pupil and help work out a strategy.

C. A child is doing poorly in school because he/she doesn't like homework. The father or mother or older sister or brother must help the child work out a homework strategy.

Other children may anonymously write "problems" on 3 x 5 cards and drop them into an "I need help" box. The entire class can discuss the problem in the counseling

format. After each session help pupils analyze their
counseling behavior to determine how well they are
listening, to discuss problems of people, and to search
for ways of coping with problems.

1.9 Who Is It?

I. Objective

A. To give students awareness of characteristic behaviors
of individuals.

II. Method

One member of the group leaves the room while the others
pick a person to be "it." The member who left the room is
called in to identify who is "it" by asking group members
to do things like the person who is "it." For example, he/she
might ask how "it" walks, talks, studies, eats, plays, etc.
Answers are given non-verbally. Several or all students
should be "it" and a large number of students should have a
chance to guess.

III. Discussion/Follow-up

Allot time for students to discuss their feelings about
certain kinds of behaviors and why certain behaviors characterize
certain people. For variation have the person who is "it" be the
person who left the room. As follow-up, have each pupil list three
or four of his/her obvious characteristics. Then have pupils
meet in pairs or small groups to "present themselves,"
seeing if the other pupils agree or would modify the list.

1.10 Who Am I?

I. Objectives

   A. To give students more self-awareness by expressing their self-images.

   B. To give students awareness of discrepancies between one's self-image and his image seen by others.

   C. To help students know each other better and to appreciate individuality.

   D. To help students recognize that some of their major characteristics may or may not be known by many of their peers.

II. Method

   A. Organizing and gathering materials. The activity requires one to four class periods. Although pencils and paper are needed, there are no right or wrong answers. Be sure students do not collaborate. Try to avoid student questions until the discussion period.

   B. Tell the students to take out a pencil and paper. Ask them, "How well do you think you know each other?" (Let them comment a few minutes.) Tell them, "We are going to see how well you know each other. Number down the left side of the paper--all the way down. Now make a list of yourself. Answer this question: 'Who am I?' Tell what kind of person you are. Make a complete list of yourself that tells 'Who am I'. (Students may ask the teacher if such and such a statement is appropriate. Merely tell them that the statements should answer the question "Who am I?")

C. Tell them, "If you want your paper read aloud, mark a 'Yes' at the top of your paper. Mark a 'No' if you do not want your paper read aloud. Now pass your papers to me."

D. From the stack of shuffled "yes" papers, pick out one paper and tell the students, "Okay, let's see how well you know each other. I'll read a list, and you can see if you know who wrote it."

E. After reading part of a list write the names of suggested students on the board. Finish the list and finish tabulating the list of suggested persons. Count the votes for each of the names suggested.

F. Tell the class the name of the student. Read other lists and proceed as before.

III. Discussion/Follow-up

Allow time for a large group discussion, some questions that might stimulate discussion include:

A. How were you able to guess who the statements were about?

B. How do people give themselves away (reveal themselves)? (Answers may be: by movements, emotions, physical expression of face, etc.)

C. What would it be like if we couldn't "read" each other a little?

D. Do you think you listed statements that are most a part of you first? Why would someone do that? (Comment: The activity lets children see themselves in the context of the whole group. They may learn that we are projecting our personality with almost every expression--physical, verbal, emotional--that we make.)

1.11 Seeing--Feeling Glasses

I. Objectives

A. To help children learn how to experience thoughts and feelings from different perspectives.

B. To help students understand that the same "fact" or event can be interpreted differently.

C. To show students that their perspective or emotional frame of reference leads to selective perception (e.g., untrusting people view people who offer to help with suspicion) and different ways of reacting to people and situations.

II. Method

Through discussion, the idea of glasses as an aid in vision is introduced as well as the term and meaning of "rose colored glasses". Ask the children to list all the different kinds of "glasses" that can be worn (e.g., suspicious, morose or gloomy, enthusiastic, caring, selfish, optimistic, pessimistic, untrusting, easily angered, threatened, etc.).

A. Set A: To help children explore and understand the concept of seeing--feeling glasses, and how general orientations (glasses people wear) influence reactions, present them short incidents such as:

1. While working on your math, a person comes and asks you for help.

2. A new child on your block asks if you want to play.
3. The teacher asks you to re-do a paper because you got a lot of problems wrong.
4. A stranger offers you a ride home.
5. A quiet student in the class finally asks you if he/she can work with you on a project.

Before reading an incident, ask students to put on different pairs of glasses. One student will respond to the incident with angry glasses, another student will respond with optimistic glasses, etc. Then read the incident aloud and have each student respond. Have the students evaluate and discuss each response and the result. Focus a discussion on the relationship between the glasses people wear and how they behave.

B. Set B: In a large group, present a situation involving two or more people. For example, two children who are new in the neighborhood are going to meet each other. One child wears suspicious glasses, the other wears enthusiastic glasses. Have the children act out their parts. Then discuss the results of the interaction (i.e., How did the two seem to get along? What were some problems?). Re-enact the play with different glasses. Vary the situations and the glasses.

Ask the pupils to think about the kinds of glasses they wear everyday and how their glasses influence their behavior. This activity may be repeated over several occasions, or each activity could explore two or three types of glasses at a time.

C. Set C: The glasses I wear. Have the children privately write about the kinds of glasses they usually wear in everyday classroom situations and their usual response. Allow the pupils to share their responses to see that different people may have different responses to the same situations.

D. Set D: Apply the glasses concept occassionally when conflict situations arise among the students. A good technique is to ask a student, "What kind of glasses were you wearing when you behaved or reacted this way?" or "What types of glasses were other people wearing at the same time?" To encourage further learning you could ask, "If you had a different kind of glasses on (such as optimistic) what would you have done and what would have happened?" The feeling-glasses technique can carry over into daily classroom life and used in "problem solving." Essentially, the technique can help children become more thoughtful about their own behavior and its consequences.

1.12 But I Can't Be Me

I. Objectives
   A. To let students feel the "loss" of free choice.

B. To let students experience giving up personal desires in a group activity.

II. Method

After the class walks around the room, have them pair off. The students in each pair then tie their adjacent (inner) legs together. The pairs then walk where they wish. After a few minutes ask the pairs to form teams of four. The adjacent legs of the four students are tied together while they stand in a line. Only the persons at both ends of each line have a free leg. Students again walk where they want to. Allow several minutes for the walking. You may wish to follow the same procedure for groups of eight.

III. Discussion/Follow-up

After the inevitable pushing, shoving, falling, and frustration, the class should discuss the problems of group activity and movement. Ask for suggestions for working in groups, in coordinating efforts, etc. As a follow-up you might have competitive tasks for the bound groups, which point up the need for cooperative and coordinated efforts even more.

Some Pointers on Writing Your Own Activities

Activities may encourage students to experience something about themselves, about others, about communication or interaction between and among people, etc. An activity may be primarily verbal or non-verbal in terms of student participation.

You might consider the following outline when you decide to develop an original activity.

A. Objective

What is the activity to accomplish? Objectives may be very subtle (to become aware of self or feelings), or quite obvious (to learn appropriate behaviors in class). Always specify what you wish the activity to accomplish. Remember, the outcome of an activity may be an internal state (feeling or emotion) or it may be an observable behavior.

B. Verbal or Non-Verbal Activity

The objective of the activity may dictate whether it is verbal or non-verbal. You should decide which kind of activity will be most appropriate to achieve the established goals.

A verbal activity, as opposed to a non-verbal activity, involves students verbally in the main part of the activity. Most activities have a verbal discussion period after the activity whether the activity was mainly verbal or non-verbal.

C. Materials

Determine if materials will be required and available for the activity. Most activities require few, if any, materials.

C. Directions

After deciding what the activity is about, it is convenient to write down specifically what you wish to tell the students about the activity, including directions and other notes that will help you.

E. Process of the Activity

Decide how to initiate the activity. You might want to make some pre-activity comments, setting the stage, for the activity.

After the activity, it may be meaningful to conduct some kind of activity extracting the essence of what has taken place. You may merely wish to make some concluding remarks, or may find that a closing discussion is as worthwhile as the activity itself. Students to process and communicate feelings, ideas, and attitudes resulting from the activity. You may think of follow-up activities that help students benefit maximally from the activity and their experiences both during and after.

You probably have often seen a need to improve communication skills among the students and/or between students and yourself. Perhaps you have seen inappropriate student behaviors that may be detrimental (physically or emotionally) to others. There may be numerous needs that might be approached by particular classroom activities.

After specifying your goals and needs, you can apply your creativity in developing activities to meet them.

2. Paper and Pencil Self-Exploration Activities

In addition to group game and activities to accomplish Level III objectives, paper and pencil activities can be used individually or in small groups. These paper and pencil activities may help pupils think about their personal values and how they

relate to other people and school situations, and may provoke
in-depth discussions further exploring the questions and issues
raised by the activities.

The objective of the following examples is to help the
teacher develop and modify activities to conform to the age levels
and cultural backgrounds of specific groups of children. Activities
such as the ones presented here can be placed into a "self-
exploration booklet," a "This Is Me" book, or individually passed
out to the children. Each activity should be introduced by the
teacher describing its rationale and purpose. Discussion and other
follow-up activities should occur after completion of each
activity. The activities need not be presented alone, but may
be incorporated into a lesson utilizing warm ups and other group
activities or games. It may be interesting to readminister
selected activities periodically to let the children examine
their own growth and development over periods of time.

2.1 About Me

Directions: Think about the questions on this page and answer
as honestly as you can.

My Name: _____ Age: _____

My Birthday: _____ Today's Date: _____

1. I was born in (town)_____ on (day)_____
   in the year_____.
2. There are _____people in my family.

3. When I'm not in school the things I like to do most are:
   A. _____
   B. _____
   C. _____
4. When I'm not in school the things I really don't like to do are:
   A. _____
   B. _____
   C. _____
5. Everybody has some things that they can do very well. The things I can do very well are:
   A. _____
   B. _____
   C. _____
6. Everybody has some things they are not so good at but which they would like to do better. The things I would really like to do better are:
   A. _____
   B. _____
   C. _____

Discussion/Follow-up

Select a particular item such as #3 and #5 for discussion to help the children get to know each other better. Then focus on the idea that everyone has positive, not so positive, and "changing" (e.g., #6) aspects about themselves.

2.2 Follow Up to "About Me"

As an exciting follow-up activity, have each child trace his body outline on paper and cut out a "life-size" outline of himself/herself. Each child would then "fill in" the outline with information from selected paper and pencil activities. The body outlines can be colored in with chalk or crayon and attractively displayed on the wall. Each child would then have an ever-changing representation of himself/herself available to classmates. This activity may help children learn that everyone has likes and dislikes, strengths and weaknesses, etc.

2.3 What Will I Be

Directions: Have you ever thought what you will be when you grow up? If you could choose, what would you choose to be?

1. The kind of job I would probably like to have is:
    A. First choice: _____
    B. Second choice: _____
    C. Third choice: _____
2. The kinds of hobbies I'd like to have would be:
    A. _____
    B. _____
    C. _____
3. Will I get married and have children? _____
4. If I did have children, what are some things I would do with them as they were growing up?
    A. _____
    B. _____
    C. _____
    D. _____
5. What might be most important to me when I grow up?
    Circle one:
    A. To have a lot of money
    B. To be famous
    C. To help other people
    D. To have a lot of friends
    E. To own a lot of things

Discussion/Follow-up

   Have the children discuss about what they'd like to be, why, etc.

2.4 What I Am Like

Part I

Directions: Suppose you could step outside of yourself and watch you. What would you see yourself doing at school and at home?

	Not Very Much	Sometimes	A Lot
1. Trying to help other kids	____	____	____
2. Getting other kids angry	____	____	____
3. Getting easily discouraged	____	____	____
4. Yelling a lot at people	____	____	____
5. Listening carefully to the teacher	____	____	____
6. Sharing things with other kids	____	____	____
7. Being friendly	____	____	____
8. Being angry	____	____	____
9. Having fun	____	____	____
10. Being very quiet	____	____	____

Part II

Directions: Now that you have looked at yourself, what do you think? Fill in the two spaces with things you are pleased about and things you would like to change.

Two things I was pleased about when I looked at me.

1. _____

Two things I would like to change.

1. _____

2. _____   2. _____

Discussion/Follow-up

Initiate discussion by mentioning that almost everyone has things about themselves they like and things they would like to change. You might ask the children to share what they like and what they would like to change.

2.5 Me and School

Directions: Everyone has feelings about school. Answer the questions carefully and honestly.

1. Here are some things in school that I do pretty well.

    A. _____
    B. _____
    C. _____
    D. _____

2. Here are some things in school that I don't do very well:

    A. _____
    B. _____
    C. _____
    D. _____

3. Here are some things that, if I could do better, would make me happier in school:

    A. _____
    B. _____
    C. _____
    D. _____

4. Circle the face that best shows how you feel about school most of the time. 😊 😐 ☹

5. When I'm in school, what kind of glasses do I usually wear (circle the word that tells about your glasses).

    Angry   Friendly   Happy   Worried/Afraid   I won't fail/
    I can do the work

    I will fail/I can't do the work

6. The kind of glasses I would most like to wear would be:

   Angry   Friendly   Happy   Worried/Afraid   I won't fail/
                                                                   I can do the work

   I will fail/I can't do the work

7. The one thing in school that I'd most like to be able to do better is:

Discussion/Follow-up

After the children have finished 2.5, you may wish to do any or all of the following.

1. Have willing children tell about their strengths and weaknesses or things they would like to become better at.

2. Have willing children discuss in pairs or small groups #7, developing suggestions or plans as to how they can accomplish their goal. Each child may write down his/her plan and find one or two children willing to help them. Follow up may involve possibilities such as one child tutoring another child, etc.

3. Ask the children to tell about their glasses (see activity on feeling glasses). This can be done in dyads, small groups or large groups.

4. Summarize the class feelings through a frequency count of responses to items such as #4 and #5.

2.6 How I Am With People In My Class

<u>Directions</u>: Let's look carefully at what you are like with other kids in this class. Read each sentence and place a check under the column that tells whether the statement is a lot like you, a little like you, or not like you.

	A Lot Like Me	A Little Like Me	Not Like Me
1. I like most of the kids in my class	_____	_____	_____
2. Most of the kids in this class are good to me	_____	_____	_____
3. Most of the time I am a helpful student	_____	_____	_____
4. I try to boss other kids around a lot	_____	_____	_____
5. Sometimes I try to do things that will make the whole class laugh	_____	_____	_____
6. Sometimes I behave like a bully	_____	_____	_____
7. I'm pretty quiet	_____	_____	_____
8. When someone needs help, I try to help them	_____	_____	_____
9. When someone gets in trouble or can't do very well, I usually make fun of them	_____	_____	_____
10. I say unpleasant or hurtful things about some kids in this class	_____	_____	_____
11. I hurt other people's feelings	_____	_____	_____

12. The one thing I do that I think makes other kids afraid of me or dislike me is:

_____

13. The one thing I do that makes other kids like me is:
    _____

14. If I could choose, here are ways that I would want other kids to see me (Circle 2 words).

    Helpful   A clown or joker   Kind   Bully   Troublemaker

    Cooperative   Tough guy   Best friend   Very popular   Good Student

15. What two things could I do that would help other kids to see me the way I would like them to see me:

    1. _____   2. _____

Discussion/Follow-up

After the children have completed this exercise, there are several follow-up possibilities:

1. Students may meet in small groups to discuss their responses to items #14 and 15. Specifically, they may try to help each other examine the value and appropriateness of their responses, giving suggestions and advice to each other.

2. Students could write contracts indicating how they will try to behave so that their peers will see them as they choose to be seen. Several days later as a follow-up, the students could discuss the degree to which they fulfilled their contracts and the results.

3. Follow-up discussions could focus topics such as "How we make friends" or on more specific topics such as "Why might some children make fun of other people (see item 9)?" "What motivates someone to be a bully?", etc.

4. Children may select items such as 14 and 15 and place them into their public presentations.

2.7 What Is Important to Me

<u>Directions</u>: Suppose you could buy things or qualities about yourself. Let's say you had $100.00. Which of these things would you buy for yourself? Write down the most money you would pay for each item.

		The Most I Would Pay For This Is
1.	To be a good student	$
2.	To have lots of people like me	$
3.	To be good in sports	$
4.	To be good in music	$
5.	To have people stop bothering me	$
6.	To be able to travel all over the world	$
7.	To be a child movie star	$
8.	To be well-behaved	$

<u>Discussion/Follow-up</u>

Before providing this list, you may wish to add or delete specific items. To vary this procedure, conduct an auction of the particular items. After the activity, have students discuss the things that are important for them, how much they would pay, why, etc.

2.8 Friends - What I Do For Them and What
They Do For Me

Directions: Each of us has friends or people we want for friends. Let's take a look at what a friend is.

1. For you, what does being a friend mean? Write down some things that a friend does for you and how a friend can make you feel.

   A. _____
   B. _____
   C. _____
   D. _____

2. Are you somebody's friends? Write down things that you do for your friends.

   A. _____
   B. _____
   C. _____
   D. _____

3. What do you think is the most important thing a friend does for you?

   _____

4. What is the most important thing or quality you have to offer your friends?

   _____

5. Circle the words or phrases below that you think make up a good friend.

   A. Tries to help you.
   B. Tries to keep you out of trouble.
   C. Plays with you.

D. Shares things with you.

E. Gives you lots of things.

F. Pushes you around.

G. Calls you names.

H. Tells you he/she will beat you up if you don't play with her/him.

I. Invites you to his/her house.

J. Talks to you and tries to make you feel better when you're upset.

K. Laughs at some of the things you do.

L. Makes fun of you.

6. What are some things that people do that tell you they are not your friend? Pick three phrases from the list above.

    1. _____ 2. _____ 3. _____

7. Do you ever have fights or arguments with a friend? _____
   How do you solve or settle your arguments? _____

Discussion/Follow-up

Several alternatives can follow.

1. Children could share and pool their impressions of what a friend means and what are the characteristics of a friend.

2. Children may discuss whether friends have arguments and how to solve arguments as well as how to make friends.

3. You may discuss needs that people have (e.g., to be loved or cared for, to feel important) or how friends can help fulfill these basic needs.

2.9 Other People and Me

<u>Directions</u>: Each of us wants people to behave in certain ways toward us. If you had your choice, how would you want people to see you and behave toward you. Use the list of words for your choices.

Happy	A tough guy	Helpful	Sad
Smart	A clown	Friendly	Kind
Angry	Sincere	Mean	Honest
A good student	A good ball player		

1. I want my teacher to see me as:

    A. _____ and B. _____

2. I want my friends to see me as:

    A. _____ and B. _____

3. I want my friends to treat me:

    A. _____ and B. _____

4. I want to be:

    A. _____ B. _____

    C. _____

<u>Discussion/Follow-up</u>

Have the children place their answers into their self-portraits. Discuss "What is a friend" and how people can make other people feel good, safe, happy, etc.

2.10 The Powers I Have--Self Control

Directions: We all have power to behave in certain ways. How do we use our power?

Self-Control: Having self-control means that we can choose not to do something even when part of us wants to. For example, we might want to answer a question but use self-control to let someone else answer the question. Also, we might be really mad at someone and want to hit them or hurt them but use self-control and do not.

1. Give an example of when you used self-control. Fill in the blanks.

    I wanted to _____ but instead I _____.

2. How is my self-control? Place a check on the line that tells about your self control.

		A lot of self-control	A little self-control	I need to improve
A.	I can take turns	_____	_____	_____
B.	I can share games, toys and other things	_____	_____	_____
C.	I cannot take other people's things or money	_____	_____	_____
D.	When I get a wrong answer, I don't feel too bad	_____	_____	_____
E.	If someone dares me to do something very dangerous, I can tell them no	_____	_____	_____
F.	I can be teased a little bit without feeling too upset	_____	_____	_____

G. I don't get too angry at other kids _____   _____   ____

3. How can using self-control help us? _____
   _____

Discussion/Follow-up

Several follow-up possibilities exist:

1. Have the children review their examples of self-control and their perceptions as to how self-control may help.

2. Have children meet in pairs or small groups to discuss their checklists. Children may try to give each other help in improving their self-control. Some children could write contracts specifying how they will try to improve their self-control. Conduct a follow-up discussion several days later to determine whether the children fulfilled their contracts and whether any benefits occurred.

2.11 The Powers I Have--Using Words

Directions: Words have a lot of power. Has anyone ever called you a name that really hurt your feelings? Has anyone ever said something that really made you feel good? You probably already know what words can mean. Let's take a closer look at how you use your power through things you say.

1. List things people say that can hurt people's feelings. The list is already started with "calling people names."
   A. Calling people names
   B. _____
   C. _____
   D. _____
   E. _____

2. List things people say that can make other people feel good.
   A. _____
   B. _____
   C. _____
   D. _____
   E. _____

3. Write an example of when you used words to make someone feel good.

   _____
   _____
   _____
   _____
   _____

4. Write an example of when you used words to hurt someone.

   _____

   _____

   How do you think your words made that person feel? _____

5. Think about how you usually use words. Answer the questions by placing a check under the words that best tell what you usually do.

	Most of the time	Sometimes	Hardly ever
A. When people help me, I say "thank you"	____	____	____
B. I call people names	____	____	____
C. When kids do things wrong, I call them stupid or laugh at them	____	____	____
D. When someone asks me to help them, I try to help them	____	____	____
E. When someone does something really well, I tell them I like what they did	____	____	____
F. When I do use words to make people feel good, I also feel good	____	____	____

6. Choices

   A. If I could start right now, I would want other people to use words in a way that would make me feel:

   _____

   B. I would use words in a way that would try to make other people feel:

   _____

Discussion/Follow-up

As previously, have children (1) review their papers, (2) further discuss how we use words, specifically name calling,

2.12 The Powers I Have--If I Were The Ruler

<u>Directions</u>: Each of us has certain powers over our behaviors. Sometimes we can choose how we will behave. Suppose you were the ruler of a very small country. How would you use your powers?

1. How would you want your subjects to feel?
   _____
   A. What would you do to make your subjects feel that way?
   _____

2. What would you do for the poor people? _____
   _____

3. How would you rule--what are three or four laws you would have?
   A. _____
   B. _____
   C. _____
   D. _____

4. What would happen to a person if that person broke a law?
   _____
   _____

5. Circle the kind of ruler you would try to be:
   A. My word would be law. Everyone would have to obey me. (Authoritarian)
   B. I would have a group of people help me to rule. We would vote on all important laws and decisions. (Democratic)
   C. I would let the people rule themselves. I would have a good time being the ruler. (Unconcerned)

6. Now, look over what you have written. Pretend you are a newspaper reporter and write a short article that tells about the ruler, how he/she rules, the types of laws there are and how the people feel about their ruler and their country.

Discussion/Follow-up

Among many follow-up possibilities for this activity are:

1. Have the children talk about their kingdoms. Discuss the value and fairness of the laws they make.

2. Discuss leadership styles (authoritarian, democratic and unconcerned), and have the children reflect upon the value of each style, how people would feel, etc. Try running a class under each leadership for a time. Have the children discuss their feelings and reactions regarding each type of leadership.

3. Discuss the choices children have when they are with other children or younger children. How do they rule? How might their rule affect others? Ask the children to list qualities of leadership style.

2.13 The Powers I Have--Group Pressure

Directions: We all have choices about the way we behave. Think about how you behave most of the time. Circle the choice that best tells what you usually do in each situation.

1. My friends dare me to do things. Some things they dare me to do are dangerous or could get me into trouble. I usually:
   A. "Take the dare" because I'm afraid the kids won't like me.
   B. Ignore the kids.
   C. Try to explain to the kids that some "dares" are just too dangerous.

2. Some of my friends don't like one classmate who seems very lonely and tries but can't make any friends. I usually:
   A. Try to make friends with the person.
   B. Go along with the other kids and ignore the person.
   C. Try to be friends with the person when my friends won't see me.

3. Some kids in the class that I like and want to be friends with are "picking on" one kid. They call the person names, pushing him around when teachers aren't looking. I usually:
   A. Ignore the situation.
   B. Join in with the kids and "pick on" the person.
   C. Tell the kids that what they are doing is hurtful.

Discussion/Follow-up

A discussion on "group pressure" may precede and follow this activity. Focus the children on considering when group pressure makes it difficult to do what "is right," or helpful and considerate.

Design or have the class design other situations and use them in succeeding "paper-and-pencil activities."

NOTE: There are no easy answers since at times we are all subject to group pressure. Perhaps it is most important to become aware that we sometimes do respond to group pressure.

2.14 This Was The Week That Was

Directions: Today is Friday, Let's take some time to think about how things went this week.

1. The best thing about school this week was _____
   _____

2. The worst thing about school this week was _____
   _____

3. School and Me this week. Circle the answer that best tells about your work or behavior:

   A. My reading was done: Poorly Ok Pretty Well Very Well
   B. My math was done: Poorly OK Pretty Well Very Well
   C. My classroom behavior was: Poor OK Pretty Good Very Good
   D. Most of the time I behaved toward other kids in a way that made them feel:

      Good   Angry   Afraid

   E. Most other kids behaved in a way that made me feel:

      Good   Angry   Afraid

   F. My teacher behaved in a way that made me feel (choose two):

      Important   Angry   Happy   Stupid   Smart

4. If the week were to start all over again, what two things would I want to have done much better:
   1. _____
   2. _____

5. For next week I think I really need to do better in:
   1. _____
   2. _____

Discussion/Follow-up

Discuss with the class how the week went including suggestions for improvement for the next week. Children may start off Monday morning by referring back to the sheet, listing what they want to improve this week. A similar activity could be used each Friday to help children more carefully examine their own behavior. For variation have partners interview each other using this form, and then spend time giving each other help.

2.15 Telegram

Directions: The telegram is an excellent way to communicate critical "feeling-type" messages. Pupils may send messages to each other, or the teacher, and the teacher may send messages to specific pupils. This technique facilitates the sharing of feelings and reactions, enhancing interpersonal communication. Copies of the following form may be dittoed to use any time or at specific time for sending messages.

Message to: _____

From: _____

You did something today that made me have an especially strong feeling and I want to tell you about it. I think you said (or did) the following _____ and it made me feel very _____.

Your classmate,

_____

Discussion/Follow-up

Individual messages need not be discussed. However, it helps to discuss how children are using the procedure and whether rules are needed about the contents of the messages. For some it helps to begin with a "happy telegram" or one limited to conveying positive feelings.

3. Discussion Approaches to Objectives

Besides non-verbal games, group interaction, and paper and pencil self-exploration activities, several different discussion approaches can use to accomplish your objectives. The procedures, presented here are (1) case or situational analysis procedures to help children discuss and explore needs, emotions, and the determinants of classroom misbehavior, (2) discussion lessons that facilitate exploration and understanding of emotions and needs and their relationship to classroom behavior, and (3) using discussion procedures to focus on classroom and human relations problems.

3.1 Case or Situation Analysis Discussion

This procedure presents the students with a written or verbal account of a particular situation or series of events which may involve literary, historical, or political characters, or persons associated with the students such as parents, teachers, or peers. After the case or situation has been presented, the class discusses particular questions about it.

Questions should focus on affective concerns such as needs, feeling, or emotions as well as the behaviors of the people in the case study. For example, the students might suggest what needs motivated a behavior of a certain individual. Questions such as "How would you feel if you were in his place?" "What might be some results of his behavior?" "What might his feelings be?" are some of the many affectively oriented questions useful in stimulating student involvement in case analysis and discussion.

In responding to student comments during a case analysis, the teacher will have numerous opportunities to convey empathy and respect. Questions should be open-ended and of a problem-solving nature rather than provoking teacher feedback of "correctness" or "incorrectness."

The analysis of cases may be made more meaningful by personalizing the discussion. In other words, students might respond to the case in terms of what they might feel or do in the situation.

During case or situation analysis discussion, students should be encouraged to practice listening skills, to offer feedback, and to develop problem-solving questions. Before a case analysis, remind the students to apply their listening skills by repeating or rephrasing the essence of a previous statement before making a comment. This type of verbal behavior also lets students know how well others understand them. Students may be reminded to offer other types of feedback such as agreement or disagreement, acceptance, etc., when appropriate.

The following are some examples of cases or situations which may be analyzed and discussed.

Case Example #1

Roy, a 6th grader, has been having trouble making good marks. He said he did well in school before he came to the present school. He likes his old school and had many friends there. He seems unhappy in his present school, finding it hard to make friends. Last week he was sent to the principal's office for throwing paper planes in the class. The principal suspended Roy for a week without really talking to him.

Questions to ask:

1. What might have been some of Roy's problems?
2. Why might his grades change greatly from one school to another?

3. What might be some of Roy's needs in the new school?
4. Was his behavior in class justified in any way? If so, in what way?
5. What would you do if you were the principal in that situation?
6. How would you feel if you were in Roy's place?

Case Example #2

In the Red Badge of Courage the young soldier found it impossible to fight when he first entered battle. He loved life and resented destroying it. He was afraid and sought personal safety. Eventually he felt guilty for withdrawing from his military duty of fighting. In time he was stimulated to make a commitment.

Questions to ask:

1. What might have led to his change in behavior?
2. Do men necessarily have to change their feelings and attitudes in order to change their behavior? Explain.
3. How would you describe the feelings of the young soldier?
4. How would you feel if you were the young soldier?
5. What would you do?

Case Example #4

Suppose a boy from a foreign country who didn't understand English too well came to your class. The teacher gave a hard lesson, saying everyone had to do it or stay after school until finished. The boy told the teacher he couldn't understand the lesson but she said he still had to do it.

Suppose someone in the class tried to help the new boy do his assignment. Then the teacher sent that person to the principal because she thought the helper was cheating.

Questions to ask:

1. How would you feel if you were in a class with students who spoke a different language?

2. How might the teacher have helped the new student?
3. What could you do to help a new student?
4. How might the new student feel when he had to see the principal?
5. If you were the principal, what would you say to the new student?

Case Example #5

A man was sent to jail for ten years because he robbed a bank. After three years in jail he escaped. He went to another part of the country and changed his name. He worked hard and saved all his money. He built a factory and paid his workers more money than any other factory. He also gave a lot of his money to hospitals to help sick people. One day a worker recognized the man and knew he was wanted by the police. Suppose the man was turned in to the police and sent to jail.

Questions to ask:

1. How might a person feel who knows that he must spend ten years in prison?
2. What are some alternatives to prison for people who have committed crimes?
3. What effects might prison have on a person?
4. Should the prisoner be required to finish his prison sentence? Why or why not?
5. What would you do if you were the judge in this case? Why?

Case Example #6

Sally is a pretty lonely 3rd grader. Nobody in class likes her. Some kids even make fun of her because she comes to school in old, dirty clothes. Sally is also not very good in math or reading. Some kids call her dumb, ugly, or stupid. Sally sometimes goes home and cries by herself because she is unhappy. Suppose Sally were in your class.

Questions to ask:

1. Have you ever felt lonely? What made you feel that way?

2. How do you feel when people make fun of you or criticize things you can't change?
3. What could the other class members do to help Sally feel better?
4. What things about a person should we consider other than his/her clothes and other material things?
5. What are some needs people have regardless of their wealth?

Concluding Comments

The previous cases are only examples for analysis and discussion. Teachers or students may develop other cases from actual past, present, or hypothetical classroom situations. Though cases based on real information and involving students or their associates may create greater interest than contrived cases, hypothetical cases may be appropriate for beginning experiences.

Case analysis activities are valuable in that they encourage systematic thought and logical reasoning that have applicability to almost any academic subject. Additionally, case analyses allow students to explore and to become more sensitive to the needs, feelings, motives, and behaviors of themselves and of others.

3.2 Lessons and Discussions to Enhance Awareness About Feelings, Needs and Human Behavior

In addition to case analyses, lessons can be introduced helping children become more aware of human feelings and needs and how these influence behavior. The following constitutes a partial listing of global objectives for such lessons.

A. To help students explore and understand their feelings and that feelings are a natural part of living.

B. To help students cope with feelings.

C. To help students become more aware of the feelings of others.

D. To help students express feelings.

E. To help students understand how their behaviors affect the feelings of others and vice versa.

F. To help students become aware of needs of themselves.

G. To help students become aware how their behaviors effect the fulfillment of the needs of themselves and others.

H. To help students explore and discuss more constructive ways of meeting the needs of themselves and others.

I. To help students use rational discussion to communicate and explore feelings and needs, and to resolve interpersonal conflicts.

Two sample units, one exploring feelings and one exploring basis human needs, will be presented as examples of discussion activities.

Unit I: Exploring Feelings

A. General Goals

A general goal of a unit on feelings is to have students explore a variety of feelings including happiness, sadness, love, anger, loneliness, anxiety (fear), and frustration. Additionally, students will hopefully learn to be more articulate in expressing their feelings, more willing to discuss these feelings, and able to act constructively upon their feelings.

B. A Sample Lesson

The following objectives could be used when discussing any feeling:

1. <u>Awareness and sharing</u>: to help children understand what the feeling or emotion is. To help children identify what provokes such feelings in themselves. To help children understand that almost everyone in the class, has experienced the feeling and/or caused another person to experience it.

2. <u>In-class behaviors and feelings</u>: To help children examine how their behavior may influence the feelings of others and vice versa.

3. <u>Understanding more about feelings and behavior</u>: To help children think about the relationship between feelings and behavior and to examine more constructive ways of behaving.

4. <u>Coping and choices</u>: To help children examine how they cope with feelings, and choices they make about when to use self-control.

5. <u>Summary activities</u>: To help pupils summarize their unique contributions and learning over the previous activities.

As an example, five lessons based on <u>exploring pleasant or happy or good feelings</u> are presented. The illustrative sample questions should be modified for specific groups of children. Each lesson would last for 15-40 minutes, depending on the ages of the students. Generally, the entire class participates and is seated in a good discussion arrangement. Each lesson may be introduced by presenting its objectives.

Series I: Pleasant Feelings, Good Feelings

Lesson #1: Awareness-sharing

    A. What does it mean to feel good or to be happy?

    B. What are some things that you do that make you feel good or happy?

    C. What are some things other people say or do that make you feel good or happy?

    D. What was helpful about today's lesson? Did you practice listening and respect? How?

Lesson #2: In-class behaviors and feelings

    A. Can you recall something another student in this room has said or done that made you feel good or happy?

B. Can you recall something you have said or done that might have made another student feel good or happy?

C. What does the teacher do that makes you feel good or happy?

What do pupils do that make the teacher feel good or happy?

D. Is it possible to feel good by saying or doing something that makes someone else feel good? Can you give an example?

E. What was helpful about today's lesson? Did we practice listening and respect for others? How?

Lesson #3: Further explorations: behavior and feelings

A. Here are some situations. What could you do to make the people feel good or happy? If you were the person, what would you want others to do?

1. Jane is very shy. Nobody plays with her or talks to her.

2. Tom is very poor. He never brings any candy or gum to school. You have a whole pack of gum.

3. A friend comes to you and is very excited; he/she wants to show you a new toy from home.

4. Sam is a new boy in class, he has been paralyzed and will always have to be in a wheelchair. Some kids don't even say hello to Sam.

5. A new girl comes to our class for a few hours a day. Some children think she is not very smart and call her names like "dummy" and "retard."

B. What was helpful about today's lesson? Did we practice listening and respect for others? How?

Lesson #4: Coping and choices

A. We all do things that make people feel happy. If you had a choice to make happy or unhappy, what would you choose and why?

B. Do we always have to try to make others happy? Do we always have to feel good or happy?

C. What are some things we can all do to try to make each other feel better or happier in this classroom?

D. What was helpful about today's lesson? Did we practice listening and respect for others? How?

Lesson #5: Summary

Several different procedures can summarize the previous lessons, such as:

A. Have the children form pairs to interview each other using the following questions:

1. What things make you feel good?

2. What do people say to you that makes you feel good?

3. What do you usually do that makes classmates feel good?

Interviewers could "present each other" to the class, or place written responses for each child on a bulletin board for other children to examine.

B. Have children list responses to critical questions such as "I usually make people feel good by . . ." These written responses may then be placed into each child's body image or placed on a bulletin board.

C. A general discussion that requests the children to recall highlights of the week's lessons can be conducted.

Other feelings such as unhappiness, sadness, anger, frustration, mixed feelings (ambivalence), etc., can be considered using the following pattern, with some variation.

A. Awareness and sharing: Discussing and examining the meaning of the feeling and what situations provoke it. For example, the following questions may be asked to initiate and guide discussion:

1. What is it like to feel angry, happy, frustrated, revengeful, lonely, rejected, etc.?

2. Can you think of a time when you felt . . .? Explain.

3. Can you think of a time when you did something that made another person feel . . .?

B. In-class behavioral feelings: Exploring how we behave in the classroom. What we do that elicits certain feelings.

1. Can you recall something a student in school might have said or done that made you feel . . .?

2. Can you recall something you might have done or said that made another student feel . . .?

3. What do teachers (the teacher) do that make you feel . . .? What do you think pupils do that make the teacher feel . . .?

C. Understanding more about feelings and behavior: Examining case analyses and hypothetical situations, asking pupils to discuss how they might feel and behave if they were in the situation, and evaluating the potential effects of their behavior (i.e., would it help solve the problem, etc.).

D. Coping and choices: Exploring how we cope with feelings, what our powers are to behave in ways to make other people have certain feelings, etc.

1. When you feel . . . what do you want to do or say?

2. If you had a choice, would you behave in a way that makes other people feel . . .?

3. Are there times when it helps to control our behavior even though we may feel very . . .? Can you give an example of when you used self-control?

4. It is sometimes helpful to tell other people or classmates when we feel . . .?

E. Summary activities.

Getting Lessons Started: Some Guidelines

1. When conducting the lessons on feelings, a basic circle or a modified circle may be appropriate for the arrangement of seats to generate closeness and to facilitate pupil to pupil communication.
2. There may be aspects of lessons which you would have the class discuss as a large group, and questions that may be more effectively considered in small groups such as mini groups, buzz groups, or dyads. Small groups or dyads may encourage children to talk about feelings. Additionally, using various groupings avoids boredom.
3. Lessons should, if possible, be scheduled for two or three times a week. A definite schedule will give you an opportunity to make some lesson preparations, and provide students with some structure and knowledge of what will be occurring.
4. To introduce a lesson, tell the students what the lesson is about; define terms that may be unclear such as "sources" or "awareness" of feelings, "coping" with feelings, etc., and, if necessary, give an appropriate example or two, to further clarify matters. To determine understanding of the topic, you may elicit an example or two from some students, or verify understanding so that the lesson may proceed with greater student participation.
5. The teacher's behaviors may be very important in stimulating student discussion. By being genuine, honest, openly expressing

feelings, and giving personal examples relevant to the discussion questions, the teacher may convey that even adults have some feelings not unlike those of children. The teacher's willingness to express thoughts and feelings in class may serve as a model for student participation and set a positive, constructive tone to each lesson.

6. During the lessons, the critical teacher behaviors presented in Section II should be used:

   A. Asking questions that encourage students to seek causes and relationships, to make suggestions, etc.

   B. Giving supportive pupil feedback, empathy, and respect and asking clarifactory questions. (This is important in securing student involvement.)

   C. Personalizing the discussion through personal anecdotes, and comments which make the lesson more meaningful.

   D. Evaluating, with the students, the process and content of the discussion, allowing everyone to take stock of what has been covered, and how it has been covered.

   E. Orienting the students to content and process objectives of the discussion, occuring before or even during the lesson when necessary.

7. During the lessons and discussion the teacher should probe when necessary, but not too deeply. Sensitivity varies from child to child so one must be careful not to tap too deeply or impress the child that the major concern is in "digging" more out rather than appreciating, accepting, and understanding his/her feelings.

8. Before and during discussions, the students may be encouraged to:

   A. listen carefully;

   B. ask questions and to seek clarification;

C. give feedback;

D. avoid interrupting;

E. avoid monopolizing the discussions.

It is also important to help students respond non-critically to each other. Students may disagree but they should not overtly chastise any pupil for his/her contribution.

9. All students should be encouraged but not pressured to participate in the discussions. Some students will readily offer comments, others will require a good deal of time before feeling comfortable, while other students will talk more freely in smaller groups.

10. Not all students will be reluctant to offer feelings and to engage in discussion. If a student should offer feelings or statements which specifically involve his/her home life, you should express acceptance but try to gently move the discussion away from home-related concerns, and focus on school-related issues, to avoid violations of privacy.

Helping Children to Understand Basic Human Needs and How Needs May Influence Behavior: A Sample Unit

Unit II: Exploring Human Needs

A. Introduction and Objectives

Human behavior is generally directed toward fulfilling basic needs. Each of us needs esteem, competence, love, attention, recognition, and so on. Much of our everyday behavior is involved in meeting our needs. Children often experience behavioral difficulties stemming from unconstructive patterns of meeting needs. While most children fulfill their needs for attention by engaging in appropriate classroom behavior, other children may gain attention through inappropriate behaviors such as defiance, clowning, etc.

A unit on exploring basic needs is to help children become aware of needs of themselves and others and to examine appropriate and inappropriate ways of meeting these needs. Such a unit must assume that children may better understand the behavior of themselves and others if they begin to comprehend the relationship between needs and behavior. The following objectives are more specific:

1. To help children become more aware of particular needs in themselves and in others.

2. To help children recognize that needs motivate behavior and to identify behaviors which they and others use to fulfill needs.

3. To help children determine the effectiveness of their need-fulfilling behaviors.

4. To help children explore effective ways of gratifying needs.

5. To help children recognize similarities and differences of the needs and the need-gratifying behaviors among people.

Prior to discussion activities focusing on understanding human needs, it might be helpful to list and describe some basic human needs. The following needs can be introduced separately or in combination.

1. <u>Psychological safety--trust</u>: The need to feel safe from physical or psychological assault, excessive criticism, or humiliation, and to feel basic dependability in people.

2. <u>Approval, attention, and affection</u>: The need to receive approval, love and affection, and attention and recognition from others.

3. <u>Need for affiliation/connectedness:</u> The need to have a feeling of belongingness with a group of people (i.e., family, friends, clubs, etc.) and to recognize similarities between one's self and others, sharing common experiences, feelings, needs, etc..

4. <u>Need for autonomy/independence/control</u>: The need to exercise basic human rights, to be free of domination, to make some choices and decisions regarding daily living.

5. <u>Need for competence/mastery/esteem</u>: The need to feel competence in academic, social, recreational, and interpersonal areas, to be able to cope with developmental tasks and life challenges, and to feel positive about one's self.

6. <u>Self-actualizing needs</u>: The need to pursue one's uniqueness, to develop one's talents and interests, to realize one's potential.

B. Developing Lessons: Some Guidelines

Each need may constitute the basic "content" of a lesson on needs. For each need a series of lessons may be developed around the following topics:

1. <u>Awareness and understanding</u>: Exploration of the need and of behaviors used to fulfill the need.

2. <u>Evaluation</u>: Assessment and discussion of the effectiveness of certain behaviors on need fulfillment.

3. <u>Alternatives</u>: Consideration of appropriate behaviors that may be used in need fulfillment.

For suggestions on seating, scheduling, eliciting participation, and strategies to employ, see the previous unit on feelings.

C. A Sample Lesson: Needs for Approval, Attention, and Affection

Lesson #1: Awareness and understanding of the need for approval, attention, and affection.

This lesson should define the need and need fulfilling behaviors used. Lesson goals might be to help students to awareness of what these needs behaviors in themselves and in others.

The following questions may be useful in pursuing the goals of this lesson. Modify these or create different ones as necessary:

A. What does it mean when someone says that people have a "need" for attention, approval, or affection? (NOTE: Students must understand these terms before discussion can be beneficial.)

B. Is there anything wrong with wanting attention, approval, or affection from others?

C. How do you feel when you don't get enough attention, approval, or affection from others?

D. What do you usually do or say to get the attention, approval, or affection of others? You may wish to give some examples for each of these needs, since behaviors may be different for each.

E. What have been some things you've done or said today to get attention or affection?

F. What are some (things done or said) by others used to fulfill their need for attention? Affection? Approval?

G. What behaviors are most used on the playground or outside of the classroom to gain attention? Affection? Approval? Your behavior? Others' behaviors?

H. What behaviors are most often used in the classroom to get attention? Affection? Approval? Your behaviors? Others' behaviors?

I. What needs might be fulfilled through acting like a "clown"?

J. What needs might a "show-off" be trying to fulfill?

K. What need or needs might a "bully" be trying to fulfill?

L. From this discussion, what can you conclude about the relationship between needs and behaviors; about the role of others in the fulfillment of your needs; and about common needs of people?

Lesson #2: Evaluation of the effectiveness of common need-fulfilling behaviors in gaining attention, approval, and affection.

This lesson should evaluate the relative effectiveness of the behaviors of self and others in the fulfillment of the needs for attention, approval, and affection. Students might begin to avoid certain behaviors which have repeatedly proved ineffective in meeting needs. The following exemplary questions might be useful in beginning the discussion. Alter questions and create others as necessary.

A. What are some examples of things you do or say that obtain the attention, approval, or affection of others without creating bad feelings toward you?

B. What are some examples of things you have done or said to obtain the attention, approval, or affection of others that caused others to have bad or negative feelings toward you? What were the reactions of others to these behaviors of yours?

C. What are some things that you have done or said or have seen others use to obtain attention, approval, and affection in class without creating bad feelings? What are some behaviors used on the playground or outside the classroom?

D. What behaviors of others usually cause you to give your attention, approval, or affection? In-class behaviors? Out-of-class behaviors?

E. What are some ways a person might evaluate the appropriateness of his/her behaviors on the fulfillment of his/her needs?

F. Can a person's behaviors satisfy needs but have some bad effects on others? Explain.

Lesson #3

This lesson should have students consider and discuss alternative behaviors effective in gaining attention, approval, and affection.

The following might be useful bases for discussions of alternative need-fulfilling behaviors.

Case A: Tom usually does poor school work and doesn't have any close friends. He talks in class when others are trying to study and frequently gets into trouble with both the teacher and students because he is so aggressive.

What might have been some of Tom's needs? What might be some acceptable ways that Tom could get attention from other students and the teacher? How might he get approval? Affection?

Case B: Sue often sits alone and seldom plays games with other kids. She tells her mother that no one in school likes her.

What appropriate and acceptable things might Sue do to have people give her attention, approval, or affection?

Case C: Roy always tries to do his best work in school, he never says anything that might cause a conflict, and he worries a lot that the teacher or a student might correct him.

This kind of behavior might be an attempt to fulfill what need? Although Roy's behaviors are not "bad," can you think of some problems with them? Are people always going to approve of everything you do? Do you think they should? Why or why not?

Case D: John doesn't have many friends and he does poorly in schoolwork. He sits in the front of the class making faces and misbehaving when the teacher is not looking.

What might be some reasons for John's behavior? What need or needs might he be trying to fulfill. What are some more acceptable behaviors that John could use?

Case E: Sara is a quiet and shy fourth grader. She helps others do their work, is always kind to people, and gives a lot, like money and toys, to others.

What need or needs might Sara be trying to fulfill? Are there some other ways to fulfill the need? Give some examples.

Case F: To convey a feeling of affection (liking) for someone, we might "tell" or show the person how we feel.

What are some things that you might do to express (show) your affection for someone?

Case G: What are some behaviors that might be used to let others know they have your attention?

The same general pattern, modifying specific questions, may be used in developing discussion lessons that consider other needs.

3.3 Spontaneous Problem Solving Discussions

The discussion behaviors, techniques, and activities presented previously provide tools and skills to enhance the problem solving and discussion capabilities of teachers and students. The true test of how well the problem solving and discussion skills have been learned comes through application to actual classroom problems.

Too often discussions are not used to assess, to consider solutions, or to evaluate the outcomes of real problems. The active involvement of students in analyzing, discussing, and resolving classroom problems may not only enhance student feelings of control and worth but may also increase the use of recommended strategies by students. Indeed, given the opportunity students often offer original and invaluable ideas towards solving problems. The involvement of students in classroom and problem solving discussions may create more positive teacher-pupil, and pupil-pupil interactions, as well as an improved learning climate.

After discussing how to approach and discuss hypothetical problems, let's focus on actual classroom problems. For organization, classroom problems may be arranged into three categories of (1) interpersonal conflicts, (2) attitudinal or behavioral problems, and (3) program planning.

Interpersonal conflicts include fights, violent arguments, hostile group rivalries, etc. Attitudinal and behavioral problems include poor work habits, negative feelings toward students or teacher, over-aggressiveness, name calling, stealing, cheating, lying, extreme passiveness, and prejudice. Finally, problems of classroom program planning include decisions about class activities, program content, project planning, or class rules.

General Goals of Spontaneous Problem Solving Discussions

General goals of spontaneous problem solving discussions might include the following:

1. to resolve the immediate interpersonal problems.
2. to help prevent similar interpersonal problems in the future.
3. to accustom students to using constructive discussion in decision making and problem solving.
4. to help students recognize and discuss particular attitudes and behaviors which could create problems.
5. to help students learn from each other better behaviors and/or attitudes.
6. to actively involve students in developing and planning classroom programs, activities, rules and procedures.

Some Guidelines for Spontaneous Problem Solving Discussions

These guidelines may be useful in conducting discussions on classroom problems, conflicts, or decisions.

Interpersonal conflicts

1. Don't threaten or force students into having problem discussions. Usually very little persuasion will be necessary to secure participation.
2. With interpersonal conflicts, determine who is actually involved. Gather the parties involved.
3. Allow "cooling off" time if necessary, then try to secure the cooperation of the students to systematically approaching the problem.
4. Encourage students to analyze the causes of the conflict from the points of view of the persons involved, the precipitating events, and what actually happened.
5. Have students explore, personally and interpersonally, their feelings, both now and during the conflict, and their needs and overt behaviors.

6. Avoid "taking sides" with either an individual or a group involved in a conflict.

7. Encourage students to suggest possible solutions to the problem.

8. Try to obtain a commitment from the individuals to carry out the agreed upon solution.

9. Have students plan for evaluating the effectiveness of the proposed solution.

10. Avoid dominating the problem solving process; be a catalyst, allowing students to resolve the problem.

11. Avoid intervention in every conflict; if possible allow students to resolve their problems without "outside" help.

12. Always secure the approval of all individuals involved in a conflict before group discussing the problem.

Attitudinal or Behavioral Problem Discussion Guidelines

1. Once you recognize attitudes or behaviors that are inappropriate, call together either the persons most involved, or the whole class.

2. Avoid moralizing ("That is a bad thing to do," etc.).

3. Introduce the problem as you see it, defining the reason for the discussions.

4. Have students comment about the issue; encourage students to share thoughts with the group.

5. Do not "dominate" the discussion; let students do most of the talking.

6. After the problem has been thoroughly discussed and defined, seek potential solutions and form a plan of action with the students.

Program or Activity Planning and Classroom Policy Making Guidelines

1. Clearly convey to students what the discussion issue is.

2. Be certain that the students know what you expect from them (i.e., "I'd like for you to offer some ideas concerning what our class project will be this month," etc.).

3. Don't ask for student suggestions unless you intend to seriously consider using them.

4. Try to involve all students in the discussion.

Discussion Formats for Spontaneous Problem Solving Discussions

Interpersonal problems, attitudinal and behavioral problems, and activity or classroom policy issues may be analyzed, discussed and even resolved through various discussion techniques. Depending upon the number of persons involved, their age and maturity, and the severity of the conflict, any one or a combination of discussion formats may be employed to relieve, or resolve the problem.

Discussion may begin in one kind of format and later move into others. The following points will tell when a certain discussion format is most appropriate.

Large group formats are quite appropriate for discussing problems which involve a large number of students or the whole class. While an interpersonal conflict usually involves only a few students, attitudinal and behavioral problems and program or activity planning may affect many and are most appropriate for the large group format. This discussion format may also be used to share the problems of a few with the whole class to demonstrate the discussion processes that may help solve problems. Additionally, large groups may gather ideas from students who have been considering problems in small groups. A large group then is useful not only as a primary format but also as a culminating format.

A dyad may be an effective discussion format when only two individuals are involved in a conflict, and are willing and intellectually capable of constructively discussing the conflict.

With young children, the teacher may need to join the dyad to ensure progress in problem solving. Some conflict discussions may be initiated in dyads, then followed through in mini groups or a large group.

Problems which involve several students might be discussed and resolved through _mini group_ discussions, or further discussed in a large group.

Role playing is useful in the discussion and resolution of problems. For example, role playing may (1) provide conflicting students with greater insight into their personal behaviors, feelings, (2) provide conflicting students with greater awareness of each other's needs, feelings, and behaviors, and (3) allow them to try out new behaviors.

Two or more students may role play at one time. The empathy and insights stimulated through role playing may be discussed in dyads, mini groups, or large groups.

Part B: Putting the Parts Together

Section III has presented at least three categories of interrelated strategies for implementing objectives in affective education:

1. Games and activities to enhance awareness and communication skills;
2. Paper and pencil activities to enhance self and other awarenesses;
3. Discussions focusing on feelings, needs, and classroom problem solving. Discussion activities were further subdivided into three categories:

A. Case analysis techniques.

B. Discussion/lessons on feelings and needs.

C. Exploring classroom problems and conflicts through group discussions.

A challenging question is how to put these three global techniques together and begin. Though much will be left to your creativity, these guidelines may help.

1. A definite time period each day or several times a week (e.g., Monday, Wednesday, and Friday) should be established for the affective activities to build continuity. Some teachers have found that the first morning period is a good time while others prefer the early afternoon. Other teachers have incorporated activities into already existing groups.

2. Start out slowly: A "starter" unit that lasts several weeks may be a useful way of beginning. The simple, direct objectives of this unit might be:

    A. To help alleviate the teacher's own anxiety and feelings of inadequacy regarding affective education.

    B. To introduce the children to some basic affective activities.

    C. To help build or reinforce basic pupil skills of communication, idea sharing, and peer cooperation.

    D. To show children that human behaviors and feelings can be discussed in an open, accepting, non-critical and non-threatening manner.

    After general "ice-breaker" type objectives, we select and introduce activities for the duration of the unit. A sequence such as the following may be selected:

    A. The first few lessons: Use activities from section 3.1 such as pantomine and gradually move to activities with children working in pairs and in groups. Be sure to explain the purpose of each activity and correlate each with a discussion. Use buzz groups for discussion as a way of generating ideas and thoughts.

B. The middle lessons: After 2-3 weeks, begin to introduce several paper and pencil activities that focus on self-exploration. First use the more simple and "safe" activities, saving those that call for greater insight for later. Again, be sure to conclude each lesson with a discussion and to occasionally vary the pace of the discussion by using large group and small group procedures.

C. The final few lessons: Use several simple case analysis techniques to introduce the children to discussion that focuses on understanding needs and human behavior. This might also be a good time to use some techniques from Section II to help the children to be more sensitive about group discussion behavior.

After completing this starter unit, you may want to initiate a unit on feelings and needs.

3. To avoid getting into a "rut," vary the lesson formats by interweaving as much as possible, activities, games, paper and pencil activities, and various discussion formats. Even though you may develop a discussion oriented unit on understanding feelings, discussion may not be the only activity. Paper and pencil activities, games, case analysis techniques and the use of dyadic, small group, and large group techniques should also be incorporated into the unit.

4. Gradually introduce conflict resolution and/or problem solving discussions. As children become more comfortable with Level III activities and more skilled in group discussion, you may gradually introduce discussions to stimulate problem solving thinking. These discussions of actual classroom difficulties should never substitute for planned Level III activities. Rather, they should be used spontaneously as needed.

5. Remember the line between affective education and psychotherapy. Affective education is to help the entire class examine human behavior, feelings, and needs. It deals with the human relations of daily classroom life. Psychotherapy focuses specifically on the private lives and problems of individual students. The line is sometimes difficult to maintain but the teacher should avoid:

A. Constantly focusing on the behavior of the same one or two students.

B. Delving into home life and matters out of the domain of the school.

C. Pushing children to reveal more information than they seem willing to offer.

D. Pressuring children to comment during discussions.

6. Participate in the activities with the children. Be a model of enthusiasm, empathy, and willingness to share your own feelings.

7. Avoid always being the center of activity. Gradually get groups of children working or discussing by themselves so they learn to communicate with each other rather than only with you.

8. Avoid falling into the trap of being a judge or moralizer. Level III activities emphasize sharing and exploring rather than listening to the teacher's views on morality or proper behavior. Empathy and respect for pupils, as well as problem solving questions, and examining behavior are crucial components of Level III activities.

With these few admonitions and guidelines, hopefully you will have enough information to begin putting some of the pieces together in your unique fashion.

Dealing with Misbehavior
by
Increasing Responsibility and Participation

Introduction

Thus far, we have focused on strategies related to affective education for all children in elementary classrooms. However, these affectively oriented activities may not be enough for some children. Certain children may evidence behavioral problems and difficulties that need more direct and systematic interventions from the classroom teacher in conjunction with the previously discussed strategies. This section presents several researched and practiced techniques for managing disturbing pupil behavior. These techniques conform to the spirit of this manual by respecting each child's feelings and needs for esteem and control through a positive, growth producing, teacher-pupil relationship.

As previously, the techniques are designed to provide sufficient information and examples to allow immediate use. However, rather than follow them "to the letter," you can modify the techniques to fit your own teaching style.

**Strategy #1: Enhancing Pupil Responsibility
By Involving Peers In Critical Teaching-Learning
And Behavioral Management Procedures**

Pupil Need to Feel Responsible

There is a saying that goes something like: "Give a person responsibility and the person will act responsibly. Take away responsibility and the person will act irresponsibly." This section examines how we can give responsibility to pupils so that their behavior and attitudes may become more responsible. Three ways of increasing pupil responsibility are: (1) involving older, well-behaving pupils in tutoring younger, less well-behaving pupils, (2) involving older, less well-behaving pupils in teaching or assisting younger children, and (3) involving well-behaving children in helping to change the behavior of their less well-behaving classmates.

A. Involving older, well-behaving pupils in the process of tutoring younger, less well-behaving children.

That all children need attention cannot be disputed. Children with behavioral and learning problems manifest even more intense needs for attention than their more "normal" peers. Indeed, many teachers say, "If I only had more time to spend with Johnny, I'm certain his behavior and learning would improve." One way to cope with this "not enough hours in the day" problem is to use slightly older children to assist younger children. This technique is a basic historical approach to our educational system, a current foundation of the British infant school system, and a major way that children learn when they are not in school. In reality, older children are constantly teaching younger children outside of school and can be a very potent source of help in school.

The list of advantages for both the older and the younger children is lengthy. Among the advantages for the younger children are:

1. The younger child receives individualized instruction and attention.

2. The younger child experiencing an appropriate child model may emulate some of the positive behaviors and attitudes of the older child.

3. The younger child can see a slightly older child as a helper and may be more receptive to help from such a person.

For older children, the advantages include:

1. The older child will have an opportunity to assume a responsible role in school.

2. The older child can practice and re-enforce basic skills through teaching a less skilled child (the best way to learn is to teach).

3. The older child will be able to experience immediate gratification in applying his knowledge to help a younger child learn.

4. The older child may examine and experience specific ways of helping and relating to younger children.

Older children can assist younger children in a variety of activities such as:

1. Reviewing math, reading, or spelling assignments.

2. Working on specific skill building activities, games, or lessons.

3. Reading stories and checking on listening comprehension.

4. Assisting a pupil in a specific project or assignment.

Guidelines For Initiating A Program

Several important guidelines and considerations in initiating a program where older children help younger children are presented below:

1. Identify one or two children in your class who can profit from tutoring from an older child. Identify, as specifically as possible, the objectives and activities you would like the child to be engaged in with the tutor.

2. Secure tutors through teachers two, three, or four grades above your class. Describe your project and its potential

benefits for the older child. In some cases the other teacher may want to use the project of helping younger children as part of a social studies program or a club activity (future teachers). Thus, the older children may be reponsible for writing reports about, or discussing problems of teaching and relating to younger children.

3. Meet with the tutor for one or two short conferences before the tutoring program begins. Use this time to discuss goals, methods, materials, procedures, and any other relevant guidelines.

4. Establish a schedule and meeting place for the older and younger children. For some children, the older child may actually come into your classroom and tutor the child in a quiet corner of the room. If this procedure would embarrass the younger child, another meeting place should be determined. For maximum benefit from the program, the older child and younger child should meet two or three times a week for twenty minute sessions.

5. Meet regularly with the tutor to discuss problems and progress, and have him/her keep some record as to what is done during each session. Also, discuss with the older child appropriate ways of relating to the younger child such as how to offer suggestions and corrections in a fair and uncritical manner. CAUTION: Do not become lax in meeting with the older child. It is definitely helpful to try to meet at least once a week for a few

minutes to discuss goals, objectives, and procedures for the coming week. Recognize that if either the older child or the younger child indicates some dislike for the working partner you may change tutors or discontinue the tutoring program for a specific child. Where there is compatibility, do not change tutors as this may inhibit the formation of a relationship between an older and younger child.

B. Involving older, less well-behaving pupils in teaching or assisting younger children.

Involvement and responsibility hold equal promise for children with learning and/or behavior problems. Oftentimes, such children may have especially strong needs to assert control, to take responsibility, and to feel constructive and helpful. While the most likely tutors may seem to be well-behaving children, tutoring may be especially constructive for some not so well-behaving children. While the advantages for the younger child are essentially the same when tutored by either well-behaving or less well-behaving older children, there are specific advantages for the older children who are experiencing behavioral or learning problems. Among these potential advantages are the following:

1. Tutoring younger children may provide the older child with esteem building success experiences through helping others.

2. A position of responsibility may elicit much more responsible and concerned behavior.

3. Through experiencing some of the problems of teachers, the older child may become more sensitive to his/her own relationships with his/her teachers.
4. Some children are reluctant to engage in remedial activities or to learn material below their age-grade level. However, these feelings may dissipate when they are asked to teach this material to younger children. Teaching is an excellent way of learning and practicing newly acquired skills.
5. The older child may learn to enjoy school more by feeling that he/she is in a position to use his/her skills to help other children, and that the teacher sees him/her in a positive and constructive manner.
6. Opportunities for channeling leadership, attention, and dominance needs into constructive outlets are provided.
7. The child may try out new and more constructive forms of behavior under non-threatening conditions. Generally, older children who do not have to be concerned about their status or image with younger children, may feel more at ease in first trying out more appropriate and helpful ways of interaction with them and later with their peers.

As a tutor, the older less well-behaving child finds a unique source of self-esteem and gratification as well as an opportunity to learn specific academic skills. Tutoring programs can be set up with the same objectives mentioned previously. Older children may tutor younger children in specific skill areas and various projects, or assist in gym instruction or playground supervision.

Guidelines For Initiating A Tutoring Program

Almost all of the guidelines mentioned in the previous section are applicable here with the following additions:

1. Take care to insure that the tutor has sufficient skill to be of some help to a younger child or to a teacher of younger children.

2. Children should not be forced into becoming tutors or teacher assistants but should be willing. If they are, a trial program may be initiated.

3. Devote at least one or two meetings to discussing with the tutor his/her responsibilities, objectives, etc. If helpful, role play a tutoring session in which you pretend that you are the student to be tutored. Have the tutor teach you or help you in a reading or math assignment for a short lesson. Observe how the tutor corrects you when you make mistakes. After the role playing session, discuss appropriate ways of helping younger children. Two children may do the role playing if both are to be tutors. Let one child role play the tutor and the other the tutee. Again, after the "lesson," discuss appropriate ways of giving help.

4. Establish a weekly meeting time with the tutors to discuss progress and problems. This is a very helpful aspect of the program as, perhaps for the first time, it will involve you and the tutors sitting down and discussing solutions to the problems that other children have! Topics from

specific teaching methods, to managing problem behavior, to the importance of conveying positive, accepting messages to the younger children, can be discussed. Not only will the children learn about effective ways of helping younger children, but these sessions may help the children examine their own behavior and attitudes.

5. Maintain communication with the co-operating teachers by meeting with these teachers at regular intervals to discuss problems and progress. Remember that there will be administrative and scheduling problems that will take time to effectively work out.

6. To maximize the potential impact of the tutoring program on both the older and the younger child, tutoring or assisting should occur regularly on an almost daily basis. Tutoring only once a week or less frequently will probably have very little impact.

7. Carefully match children as appropriately as possible. Generally, an age difference of at least two to three years will help minimize feelings of rivalry between the tutor and the tutee. Also, the tutor should have at least as many skills in the subject he/she is tutoring as the tutee. Again, it will be important to determine the compatibility of the two children, recognizing that some may not get along well.

Some Illustrations

These examples are intended to clarify the application of cross-age teaching, using both <u>well-behaving</u> and <u>poorly-behaving</u> pupils as tutors. In each case, at least one teacher had the responsibility of "supervising" the tutor.

1. Josh, a sixth grader, was reading at a high fourth grade level. He could not read the same books that his classmates read, but he refused to read books that were below the level of his classmates.

    <u>Problem</u>: How can Josh's teacher get him to read fourth grade level material, experience success, and improve reading abilities when he refuses to read "little kids" books?

    <u>Strategy</u>: Josh's teacher implemented a cross-age teaching program where Josh tutored a fourth grade girl in reading for three 20 minute sessions per week. Josh met with the fourth grade teacher every Friday to review <u>his</u> student's progress. This situation Josh enabled to learn without losing face and to see himself as a responsible student.

2. When attending summer school, Harry was placed in an ungraded class. Having little interest in reading, Harry would try to help the younger children with their lessons instead of doing his reading. Harry was criticized for interacting with and helping younger children and for not working.

    <u>Problem</u>: How can Harry's desire to interact and help younger children be used to facilitate his own progress

in reading?

Strategy: To allow Harry to gain esteem rather than criticism, the teacher arranged for Harry to tutor a younger child in reading for fifteen minutes each day. Once a week his teacher reviewed what he was doing and discussed the program with him. Not only did Harry become more interested in his own reading, but he also started to come to school earlier so he could finish his own work, thereby leaving more time to work with the younger child.

3. Janice, a sixth grader, was older and more physically mature than most of her peers. Janice was also having trouble learning arithmetic since she did not identify with her peers. She ignored all attempts by her teacher to teach her arithmetic either as a member of the class or individually.

Problem: Janice was not learning arithmetic to the point of possible failure. Unless pushed to participate in math class, Janice was not a behavior problem. The teacher needed to find a way to motivate learning without creating a behavioral disruption.

Strategy: Janice's teacher asked her if she would care to teach some younger children in the third grade. Janice was very excited about the prospects of teaching and playing the role of an older person. She began teaching a group of three third graders arithmetic every day for twenty minutes. In addition, her teacher secured an eighth grader to tutor her in sixth grade arithmetic. Janice accepted instruction from the eighth grader because she wanted to learn enough arithmetic to keep teaching her third grade "class."

4. Mrs. Whitter's fifth grade class began a social studies unit on "Helping Roles in Society." The class split into groups, to try to experience and report on a helping role. One group chose teaching. Mrs. Whitter asked around and found that a kindergarten teacher had a group of children who had problems with reading readiness skills. The kindergarten teacher offered to train this fifth grade group in how to teach some of the necessary readiness skills. The fifth graders started tutoring the kindergarten children for fifteen minutes a day, meeting once a week with each teacher to discuss their students' progress, and to receive hints on teaching methods.

When their social studies unit was finished, they wrote up a report and presented it to their class. They also requested that they be able to meet with their kindergarten children at least once a week for the rest of the semester even though the project was over.

5. Chris, a fifth grader, had just transferred to a new school system in a different state. His previous fifth grade class was working on approximately the same levels as his new class in all subjects except arithmetic. In arithmetic, Chris's old class was a year behind his new class. Even though Chris was a good student, he found

himself behind his new classmates. To help him "catch up," Chris's teacher had him tutor one of the fourth graders at the school. Meeting daily with the younger child, Chris was motivated to be "one step ahead" of his tutee and thus found himself catching up with his regular class. Chris's teacher created a situation in which Chris would gain esteem, rather than experience failure in a class where he would be behind his peers.

C. Involving well-behaving children in helping to change the behavior of their less well-behaving peers.

In believing that the classroom teacher must solve all behavior problems in the classroom, we sometimes overlook the fact that the peer group often has powers more dynamic and forceful than the teacher's. Quite often peer power to control pupil behavior is used negatively. For example, children will often encourage and support the disruptive misbehavior of one or two of their classmates for diversion from classroom routine. At other times, children may encourage misbehavior as a means of subverting teacher authority, or to meet personal needs for control and dominance.

While peer group can influence behavior unconstructively, it can also be used constructively to influence behavior. The basic issue is to re-channel the behavior and attitudes of peers in their responses to "problem" children in the classroom. It is important to alert the peer group to their power and to help them realize that they have basic choices as to how they can exert their power. They can use their power to ignore, to encourage misbehavior, or to encourage appropriate behavior. Three general strategies

are presented for involving peer groups in changing the behavior
of peers with specific learning or behavior problems.

1. Confrontation: Let us say that any of the following
   problems have been occurring in the classroom:

   A. One or two pupils are consistently rejected or ignored
      by their peers to the point that the rejected children
      feel unliked or isolated.

   B. One or two children are continually "picked on" by
      other children who call them hurtful names or
      scorn them for differences (wearing glasses, having
      a physical handicap, demonstrating immature behavior,
      etc.).

   C. One or two children are continually misbehaving to
      acquire peer attention (laughter).

   D. One or two children continually fail to complete
      their work, wander about the room, disrupt or
      "bother" other children.

   In any of these cases you may find that you react as
   an arbitrator or a disciplinarian. You may spend a great
   deal of time trying to manage behavior and become caught
   in a power conflict between your ideas of appropriate
   classroom and interpersonal behavior and what the children
   in the classroom are subtly encouraging or supporting.

   Through observation you may find the children who
   most influence the "problem" children. An informal
   meeting with these children or the entire class help
   the children become aware of how they are using their
   power and what choice they have. The discussion may focus
   on any or all of the following issues:

   (1) How are we influencing the behavior of the
       person involved?

   (2) Are we using our power to ignore, encourage
       misbehavior, or support appropriate behavior?

(3) How do you think the person(s) feel about our response?

(4) If you had a choice would you choose to ignore, encourage misbehavior, or support more appropriate behavior? What impact would your choice have on the person? If you were that person, how would you want others to respond to you?

Following this initial discussion, the children may be asked to offer suggestions as to what they could do to support more appropriate behavior rather than encourage misbehavior. Each child may be asked, if he/she wishes, to state a plan that he/she could use in future responses to the child's misbehavior. The merits of each suggestion may be discussed. You may ask children to write a contract or statement as to how they will strive to interact with the particular child. Conduct several follow-up meetings with the group to determine progress and problems. Reward the children with praise when they demonstrate more constructive approaches to the problem child.

Illustration

Michael, an eight year old third grader exhibited very bizarre behaviors such as hiding in the coat closet, crawling under, or standing on top of his desk. These unpredictable behaviors might occur at any time, and were encouraged by the laughter of Michael's classmates. Also, Michael was falling behind in completing his assignments. Michael saw the third grade counselor onee a week but there was little change in his behavior.

When Michael entered the fourth grade, his academic performance deteriorated more with little behavioral improvement. There was a group of boys who enjoyed watching Michael's misbehavior. The teacher had a private meeting with these boys. To relieve the tension and anxiety in the meeting, the teacher started by asking how blind children learn to read. The children talked about having to use braille materials and special procedures. After that brief discussion, the teacher led into a discussion of whether the group could do something special for Michael to help him learn and behave more appropriately. Although the children laughed at Mike's behavior, the teacher accepted this laughter as normal anxiety and then asked the children if they were encouraging Mike to misbehave or supporting constructive behavior. Deciding to help Michael, the children discussed specific ways of helping. Each child in the group decided not to laugh at Mike but to warn him that he wasn't going to get his work done and that he was going to get in trouble. Each child also "took on" a specific project. One decided to play with Michael each day at lunch. Another decided to help Mike each day in reading, etc.

The teacher concluded the meeting by asking each child to restate his commitment, and to begin the special program the next day. She also set up a time at the end of the next day for a follow-up meeting to discuss problems and progress. Gradually the program began to take effect and have a positive influence on Mike. The boys responded helpfully, continuing to encourage Mike in more appropriate classroom behavior. Mike's bizarre behaviors diminished steadily as he received more appropriate peer attention and interaction. To maintain the new peer group strategy, the teacher held weekly meetings with the boys to check on their response and to give encouragement and support.

In this case, confronting certain peer group members with how they were using their power of influence was a most effective strategy. Instead of setting up a battlefield where the strongest would win (teachers often lose such battles), the teacher formed an alliance to help solve a very real problem. The teacher also helped each child develop a clear strategy or alternative way of responding to the "problem" child. Thus, the use of a confrontation strategy involves at least four critical elements:

(1) Observing how certain peers are affecting the misbehavior of the student.
(2) Confronting the peers with choices as to how they will use their power.
(3) Helping peers to respond in ways that will encourage more appropriate behavior.
(4) Conducting follow-up meetings to discuss the problem, to evaluate the effects of new strategies, and to praise the children for their participation.

Before concluding "confrontation," realize that there may be situations where the peer group is virtually powerless to influence the behavior of one of their classmates. This may occur when the "disturbing" child is physically domineering the other children. In such cases, well-behaving peers may be afraid and unable to influence the misbehaving child. Here, we may need more direct techniques such as a reward or contracting system (see next section) or to channel the child's possible control needs into more constructive outlets, such as being a tutor or assistant teacher.

In addition to confronting peers with their power and using it to aid in behavior management, two other general strategies may be useful; the buddy system and the entire class helping project.

2. Buddy System: The buddy system may be particularly helpful for shy, isolated children, or children who have some difficulty in following directions and working independently. The buddy system is rather direct, involving any or all of the following:

   A. The well-behaving "buddy" can give immediate help, answer questions, and interpret directions. The buddy may even encourage and support to keep his/her partner work oriented. Before children begin on their assignments, the buddy makes sure that his/her partner clearly understands the task to be done.

   B. The buddy helps his/her partner on the playground or during free-time activities. The buddy may take initiative to play games or do other activities with his/her partner.

C. The buddy is a reality agent for the child. When the child begins to lose interest, show frustration, or become excessively angry, the buddy intervenes and offers immediate help in redirecting his/her partner to the appropriate task.

D. The buddy meets at regular intervals during the school day to check on the progress of his/her partner.

A buddy system may be initiated by a conversation with the problem child to determine if the child would like to work more closely with another pupil. Where possible, it helps to have the pupil identify one or two people he/she would like to have as "buddies." After being nominated, they should be asked whether or not they would like to participate in the buddy program. You may then meet only with the helper to determine the nature and manner of help to be given, or you may meet with both children simultaneously and have them discuss the nature and manner of help.

A helpful variation of a buddy system is to combine it with a particular reward or incentive system explained in the next section. For example, a child with learning or behavior problems may develop a "work contract" specifying the behavior to be engaged in and the assignments to be completed. Also, the child may rely on specific forms of help from the buddy. After completing the work (fulfills the contract), the child and the buddy would receive a reward such as being given time to play a game or work on a project together, etc. As with other peer helping programs, you should meet regularly to discuss problems and progress and to help refine procedures.

3. The entire class helping project: An effective "ice-breaker" for peer helping programs is to have the entire class assist each other rather than to isolate several needy children. Several class periods may be needed to develop and evaluate such a program. One way to start is with a paper and pencil exercise with each child listing an area of learning or behavior that he/she could probably improve in (e.g., doing better in spelling, getting into fewer arguments, etc.). After listing their "problem" area or areas, the children meet in pairs to help each other accomplish their goals.

This project would have at least four phases of activity. The first phase, identifying the problem, might be accomplished by a paper and pencil activity. The second phase would be to set up a clearly stated goal (e.g., to get a score of 90% or better on my next spelling test, to complete all my daily arithmetic assignments, to engage in recess activities without fighting, or to play with a group at recess instead of staying by myself). The third phase would be to identify ways of accomplishing the goal and find ways that the "buddy" or assistant can help to accomplish the goal. The final phase would be to determine whether the child accomplished the goals. The children work as partners during all four phases to assist each other in accomplishing their goals. During this project, lasting one day or longer, the children could give progress reports to inform their classmates as to the nature of their projects.

After these projects, the children may go on to other projects or aspects of their behavior or they may wish to drop the technique. This technique may help to legitimize more specific peer helping programs such as <u>confrontation</u> or <u>buddy systems</u>. The essential message conveyed through the entire class method is that it is wholly legitimate to get help in accomplishing a personal behavior change. It would help if the teacher also engaged in a change project.

Before preceding, let's recapitulate the importance of planning and supervision in establishing any type of peer helping program. Carefully provide the children with ample direction and clarity and help them examine increasingly more constructive ways of helping other children. Remember, rarely will any peer helping program become an instant success.

4.2 Strategy #2: Individualizing Learning and Behavior Management Through Learning Contracts

Introduction: In any classroom there may be several children whose academic performance and/or classroom behavior is consistently below par. One way to improve the performance of such children is through individual learning contracts. Briefly, a learning contract is a clearly (written) agreement between teacher and pupil specifying at least three essential elements: (1) the task the child is to complete or the desired behavior, (2) the reward the child will receive, and (3) any special conditions such as where the task or how the task is to be completed (alone, with a buddy, etc.) and when the reward will be received.

The principal advantage of learning contracts is that they provide a specific and effective guideline for each pupil. Pupils with learning or behavior difficulties often do not understand basic rules of personal conduct (i.e., people should not fight, students should work quietly in class, finish tasks that are started, etc.). Such children may need a much clearer prescription of what is expected of them and may initially need more systematic rewards as an incentive to complete tasks or to maintain certain behavior. Learning contracts provide both understanding of specific target behaviors and incentives for pupils. Let's take a closer look at the essential elements of a learning contract, examine some sample contracts, and then examine some guidelines for establishing contracts.

I. <u>Elements of the Learning Contract</u>: As mentioned, a learning contract specifies at least three ingredients; **task**, reward, and conditions. These ingredients are more clearly described below.

   A. <u>The task</u>. The learning task to complete or the behavior to strive for must be clearly stated to provide a "map" for the child. The following are examples:

   1. Correctly complete ten math problem in 30 minutes.
   2. Read the first three pages of the following story... Answer correctly 4 of the 5 comprehension questions by 10:30 a.m.
   3. Participate in the social studies discussion without getting out of your seat.
   4. Complete the recess period after lunch without getting into a fight.
   5. Volunteer and give your best answer twice during the science lesson.
   6. Complete and hand in all assignments in math and reading by noon and correct all errors by 2:00 p.m.
   7. Participate in today's recess and other activities without calling anyone a derrogatory name.

   Though tasks to be completed are clearly stated, these tasks are typically quite individualized. For instance, in the first example, most of the class members may have more difficult problem to complete. As well as being clear, each task must be geared to the child's level of knowledge and skill. Also, since some children have a

144

history of failure, feelings of incompetence, and
generally negative reactions to academic work, we want
to help them develop more positive feelings about their
abilities. So, we may also want to __initially__ make the
tasks short and simple enough so that the child can
easily accomplish the task and begin to experience some
success. Gradually, the tasks should become more lengthy
and more difficult.

B. The reward. In classrooms, we use grades or teacher praise
as rewards for appropriate pupil performance. Most
children are anxious to please the teacher and to receive
praise. Others react to the challenges of learning and
need little teacher reinforcement. However, other children
attribute little meaning to grades or praise or they
cannot wait for rewards that come at the end of the day,
week, or at the end of a marking period. These children,
in addition to clearly defined tasks, may also need
clearly defined individual rewards. We may assume that
this will help the child to complete the task. Hopefully,
in time, the reward will become less important to the
child than completing the task successfully. Let's look
at two general types of rewards, symbolic rewards and
tangible rewards.

1. Symbolic rewards. Symbolic rewards, the most frequently
    used rewards, include praise from the teacher, grades,
    gold stars, and smiling faces. Although these rewards,
    have little tangible value, most children attribute

value to them. However, for some, an "A" or a gold star is relatively meaningless and certainly not powerful enough to be an incentive since these children have learned that their chances of obtaining such rewards are slim. It may help to make symbolic rewards more available and frequent through appropriate learning tasks. However, some children need more concrete rewards.

2. <u>Concrete rewards</u>. We can divide concrete rewards into (a) privileges, and (b) tangible items.

   a. <u>Privileges</u>. A wide range of privileges can be made available to children.

   (1) watering plants
   (2) feeding animals
   (3) cleaning chalkboard
   (4) free time to color, play a game, work on a project
   (5) running a special errand
   (6) reading a story to a younger group of children
   (7) staying after school to help the teacher
   (8) constructing a bulletin board
   (9) working with another child on a project
   (10) going to the office and helping the secretary run the ditto machine
   (11) serving as an assistant to the custodian
   (12) working in the kitchen
   (13) listening to the radio

   b. <u>Tangible items</u>. When symbolic rewards and privileges don't have an impact, tangible items may be used. Children may "work for" items such as candy, gum, crayons, pencils, comic books, a doll, movie tickets, green stamps, etc. Children may even earn points or tokens for completing specific work, thus introducing the concept of banking or postponing rewards. For example, a child may receive 1 point for completing each assignment and save these points to buy various items (i.e., candy bar = 10 points; movie ticket = 100 points; box of crayons = 50 points; etc.). Thus, while the tangible rewards may be received only once a day or once a week, the child will receive symbolic rewards much more frequently.

Sometimes parents can contract a program that involves delivering rewards at home through some tangible item or granting of a specific privilege. The critical ingredient here is that the contract must involve three people; the child, the parent, and the teacher. Moreover, the teacher must send frequent and systematic records home to let the parent know whether or not the child fulfilled his/her part of the contract.

Whether using symbolic or concrete rewards, it should be remembered that the child should help decide what the reward will be and when it will be given. This helps the child develop a greater sense of commitment and participation in the program, and allows the teacher to find meaningful rewards. Furthermore, we must be realistic as to how much of a change a reward program will yield. While research shows that carefully designed reward programs are quite beneficial, change rarely comes overnight. The child's tasks must be individualized and the teacher must look for small increments rather than immediate and dramatic changes.

    c. <u>Conditions</u>. The third essential element, in addition to specifying the task and the reward, is to stipulate any additional conditions that might help to clarify the contract for the child. Among these additional conditions might be:

      (1) where the child is to do the work (at desk, in library, etc.)
      (2) whether the task is to be done independently
      (3) who the child should see when he/she needs help
      (4) when will the reward be given
      (5) will the child have a chance to correct mistakes, be required to correct mistakes, etc.

II. <u>Sample Contracts</u>: Here are several examples of a relatively simple contract focusing on one task or one behavior. Others are more complex.

    A. This contract is a daily contract for a child who rarely completes academic tasks. Each morning the teacher and child "reaffirm" the contract. Gradually, the tasks become greater and the rewards become more infrequent.

Task

   Complete ten math problems by 9:30 a.m.
   and any corrections completed by 9:45 a.m.

Reward

   You may choose one of the following:
   1. Time to color or play a game until
      10:00 a.m.
   2. One piece of gum to be received right
      after lunch.

Conditions

   1. Work independently at your desk.
   2. If you get stuck raise your hand and the
      teacher will come over to help. If the
      teacher doesn't come right away, go on
      to the next problem.

Signed: _____(Student)

        _____(Teacher)

B. In this contract a point system has been introduced to help delay rewards and the assignments have increased.

Task

Complete the morning's math and reading assignments and correct any errors by 11:00 a.m.

Reward

You may choose one of the following:
1. Five points to be "banked" towards a prize at end of the week (the prize list must already be known).
2. Fifteen minutes at the end of day to work on project with your partner.
3. Go down to the office and help secretary run off dittos from 11:45-12:00 noon.

Conditions

1. Work in your assigned area.
2. If you need help, raise your hand or come up to my desk.
3. When your work is complete, bring it to me by 10:30 a.m. to be corrected.

Signed: _____(Student)

_____(Teacher)

C. This contract focuses both on work to complete as well as appropriate classroom discussion behaviors. The child may earn points to cash in either at the end of the day or later.

Task

1. Complete afternoon social studies assignment.
2. Participate in the discussion without interrupting others. Raise your hand and wait until you are recognized by the teacher before you talk.

Reward

1. Five points for completing your assignment. You will also receive a two-point bonus for neatness.

2. One point for each time you raise your hand and are recognized by the teacher before you talk.

Conditions

1. Social studies can be done with a partner.
2. Work as quietly as possible.
3. During the group discussion, you must remain seated.
4. Points may be cashed in at end of day or at a later time.

Signed: _____(Student)

_____(Teacher)

D. This contract for an entire week's work and with delayed reward, indicates that the child has had previous contracts.

Task

1. Complete daily assignments in reading and math for entire week.
2. Participate in playground activities during recess without fighting.

Reward

1. Five points for each day's math assignments.
2. Five points for each day's reading assignments.
3. Five points for participating in playground activity without fighting.

Conditions

1. To receive points for reading or math assignments, you must be 80% correct. You can correct your work.

> 2. Reward can be collected Friday afternoon. You can "cash in" your points for any of the following list of privileges (e.g., 25 points = 1 comic book; 25 points = water plants for one week; 1 green stamp for each point, etc.).
>
> Signed: _____(Student)
>
> _____(Teacher)

III. Some guidelines for beginning contract programs with children.

A. **Begin in small steps.** Instead of involving the entire day's tasks, start small by focusing on one aspect such as reading or math. This will allow you and the child to gain experience and comfort with contracts which can be easily expanded to include more and more tasks.

B. **Involve the child.** Involving the child as much as possible in designing the contract helps him/her to feel more responsible with regard to fulfilling the contract. Eventually, some children may be able to design their own contracts.

C. **Be systematic.** Make certain that you deliver the rewards as contracted. A danger coming from quick improvement in the child's performance is the teacher's becoming less systematic or even forgetting about the contract. The child may then revert to less appropriate performance.

D. **Don't give up too soon.** It may take the child a while before he/she understands the contract approach or before an appropriate contract is developed. Thus, instant changes should not be expected. If the child does not seem to "catch on" after several days, revise the contract. Perhaps the tasks and/or the rewards will have to be revised.

E. <u>Involve parents where possible</u>. As mentioned earlier, parents can be vital in a contract program. For example, contracts can be devised where parents reward their children (allowances, special privileges, etc.) for completing specified tasks or for maintaining appropriate levels of behavior in school.

F. <u>The contract method can be expanded</u>. If other children in the class become interested in learning contracts, they can write contracts for specific projects even for grades in various subjects. Of course, these children will not need concrete rewards since symbolic rewards (i.e., praise, grades, etc.) will be sufficient.

G. <u>What if classmates resent one or two children receiving tangible rewards</u>? Through frank and serious discussions of human behavior and needs try to help the children understand that some children really do need extra help and special efforts to help them learn. Also you may help the children explore the types of rewards they already receive in the classroom, or let them experiment with a contract program using privileges or symbolic rewards.

H. **Merge the contract and buddy system.** Sometimes it helps for the "problem" child to have a buddy as an assistant. Buddy procedures can be planned into the contract. If care is taken, the buddy can also correct work and dispense checkmarks or points. Indeed, the child and the buddy may both receive a reward when the child fulfills the contract.